D1017543

TARGETS AND INDICATORS

POLICY ANALYSES IN INTERNATIONAL ECONOMICS 22

TARGETS AND INDICATORS: A BLUEPRINT FOR THE INTERNATIONAL COORDINATION OF ECONOMIC POLICY

John Williamson
Marcus H. Miller

INSTITUTE FOR INTERNATIONAL ECONOMICS
WASHINGTON, DC
SEPTEMBER 1987

John Williamson is a Senior Fellow at the Institute for International Economics. He was formerly economics professor at Pontifícia Universidade Católica do Rio de Janeiro, University of Warwick, Massachusetts Institute of Technology, University of York, and Princeton University; Advisor to the International Monetary Fund; and Economic Consultant to Her Majesty's Treasury. Williamson has published numerous studies on international monetary issues, including Political Economy and International Money, IMF Conditionality, *and* The Failure of World Monetary Reform 1971–74.

Marcus H. Miller, a Visiting Fellow at the Institute, is Professor of Economics and Director of the Parliamentary Unit at the University of Warwick. He has been an advisor to the Treasury Committee of the House of Commons (1981) and a Houblon Norman Fellow at the Bank of England (1982), and is currently joint program director in international macroeconomics at the Centre for Economic Policy Research, London.

The authors acknowledge with gratitude the collaboration of Hali J. Edison in an earlier study that helped lay the basis for this paper; stimulating interchanges with Ronald I. McKinnon and James Meade; the research assistance of Mehrdad Emadi-Moghadam and Mark Sagrans; numerous invaluable comments on earlier drafts by seminar participants, referees, and colleagues; and the typing of Debby McGuire. J.W. and M.H.M.

INSTITUTE FOR INTERNATIONAL ECONOMICS
11 Dupont Circle, NW
Washington, DC 20036
(202) 328–9000 Telex: 248329 CEIP Fax: (202) 328–5432

C. Fred Bergsten, *Director*
Kathleen A. Lynch, *Director of Publications*
Ann L. Beasley, *Production Manager*

The Institute for International Economics was created, and is principally funded, by the German Marshall Fund of the United States.

The views expressed in this publication are those of the authors. This publication is part of the overall program of the Institute, as endorsed by its Board of Directors, but does not necessarily reflect the views of individual members of the Board or the Advisory Committee.

Library of Congress Cataloging-in-Publication Data
Williamson, John, 1937–Targets and indicators.
(Policy analyses in international economics; 22)
''September 1987.'' Bibliography: p. 106.
1. International finance. 2. International economic realtions. 3. Economic policy. I. Miller,
M.H. (Marcus H.) II. Title. III. Series.
HG3881.W4936 1987   332.4′5   87–22724

ISBN 0–88132–051–x

Contents

6 CONCLUDING REMARKS *page 64*

APPENDICES

TABLES

FIGURES

Preface

The research program of the Institute has devoted considerable attention to the functioning of the international monetary system, particularly in developing the concept of target zones as an alternative to the regime of floating exchange rates which has prevailed for most of the period since 1973. We believe that the establishment and existence of effective global monetary arrangements is of critical importance, to underpin a stable and growing world economy and to provide the basis for open trading arrangements. We further believe that the inadequacies of floating rates in all these respects have become increasingly apparent in the 1980s, and that it is imperative to consider alternative possibilities.

The present study extends the Institute's work in this area in three important ways. First, it attempts to link the target zone idea with the "indicators" approach agreed by the major industrial countries at the Tokyo (1986) and Venice (1987) summit meetings, developing a comprehensive set of possible guidelines for management of the monetary system in the future. Second, it tries to give some idea of how these guidelines would have worked in practice had they been in place during the 1980s. Third, it compares the proposed regime with past international monetary arrangements and other suggestions for the future, to see how the alternative possibilities would seem to fare against a set of common criteria. In doing so, the study attempts to take account of the summit innovations and the apparent movement toward adoption of "reference ranges"—a variant of the target zone approach—by the major countries since late 1986 and early 1987.

The Institute for International Economics is a private nonprofit research institution for the study and discussion of international economic policy. Its purpose is to analyze important issues in that area, and to develop and communicate practical new approaches for dealing with them. The Institute is completely nonpartisan.

The Institute was created by a generous commitment of funds from the German Marshall Fund of the United States in 1981, and continues to receive substantial support from that source. This study was partially supported by the National Institute for Research Advancement in Japan, whose help is greatly appreciated. Major institutional grants are also being received from the Ford Foundation, the William and Flora Hewlett Foundation, and the Alfred P. Sloan Foundation. A number of other foundations and private corporations are contributing to the increasing diversification of the Institute's financial resources.

The Board of Directors bears overall responsibility for the Institute and gives general guidance and approval to its research program—including identification of topics that are likely to become important to international economic policymakers over the medium run (generally, one to three years) and which thus should be addressed by the Institute. The Director, working closely with the staff and outside Advisory Committee, is responsible for the development of particular projects and makes the final decision to publish an individual study.

The Institute hopes that its studies and other activities will contribute to building a stronger foundation for international economic policy around the world. Comments as to how it can best do so are invited from readers of these publications.

C. FRED BERGSTEN
Director
August 1987

1 Introduction

This study is a response to the initiative launched at the Tokyo summit in 1986 to try to construct an indicator system to guide the international coordination of macroeconomic policies. It develops a comprehensive set of proposals, summarized in the box (overleaf).

This "blueprint" includes the target zone proposal for exchange rate management, developed at our Institute in 1983 when the fashion for free floating was at its zenith (Bergsten and Williamson 1983, Williamson 1985). It supplements that proposal by a formula for the growth of domestic nominal demand calculated to support stable, noninflationary growth. It includes principles that should govern monetary and fiscal policy in each country to enable them to pursue simultaneously the intermediate targets for both domestic demand and the exchange rate.

Official views on the need for international macroeconomic policy coordination have changed radically since 1983. The last gasp of the old orthodoxy was the Group of Ten (G-10) Report published in June 1985, which stated that "the majority of the Deputies, therefore, agree that the adoption of target zones is undesirable and in any case impractical in current circumstances" (G-10 1985, para. 32). Three months later the Group of Five (G-5) met at the Plaza, agreed that the value of the dollar was higher than could be justified by fundamental economic conditions, and subsequently started to intervene in the exchange markets and modify their interest rates to push the dollar down.

The Tokyo summit of May 1986 appeared to reject the target zone proposal, and plumped instead for developing a set of indicators as a basis for comprehensive macroeconomic policy coordination. Paradoxically, however, in the following months most of the emphasis in international negotiations was on exchange rates. The Baker-Miyazawa Agreement in October 1986 first suggested that the authorities on both sides felt that the dollar had fallen enough. After a further decline, the Louvre accord of February 1987 by the "G-6" (the Group of Seven less Italy) declared that the existing pattern of

1

The Blueprint

The participating countries [the Group of Seven] agree that they will conduct their macroeconomic policies with a view to pursuing the following two intermediate targets:

(1) A rate of growth of domestic demand in each country calculated according to a formula designed to promote the fastest growth of output consistent with gradual reduction of inflation to an acceptable level and agreed adjustment of the current account of the balance of payments.

(2) A real effective exchange rate that will not deviate by more than [10] percent from an internationally agreed estimate of the "fundamental equilibrium exchange rate," the rate estimated to be consistent with simultaneous internal and external balance in the medium term.

To that end, the participants agree that they will modify their monetary and fiscal policies according to the following principles:

(A) The *average level* of world (real) short-term interest rates should be revised up (down) if aggregate growth of nominal income is threatening to exceed (fall short of) the sum of the target growth of nominal demand for the participating countries.

(B) *Differences* in short-term interest rates among countries should be revised when necessary to supplement intervention in the exchange markets to prevent the deviation of currencies from their target ranges.

(C) National *fiscal policies* should be revised with a view to achieving national target rates of growth of domestic demand.

The rules (A) to (C) should be constrained by the medium-term objectives of maintaining the real interest rate in its historically normal range and of avoiding an increasing or excessive ratio of public debt to GNP.

exchange rates was "broadly consistent with underlying economic fundamentals."

Although the communiqué following the Louvre did not announce the fact, it seems that the finance ministers agreed at that meeting to rather precisely defined "reference ranges" for their exchange rates. These appear to differ from the proposals for "target zones" developed in Williamson (1985) in five important respects: the ranges have not been publicly announced; the bands are narrower; they are defined in terms of nominal bilateral rates against the dollar rather than real effective exchange rates; they have a provisional, "until further notice," flavor; and the obligation when a rate reaches the edge of its range is to consult rather than to implement a prespecified policy reaction.

Despite these differences from Williamson's earlier proposals, which do in our view carry with them certain dangers and disadvantages that are discussed further in the concluding section of this study, we welcome the remarkable progress that has been made in returning to a structured exchange rate system over the past two years. At the same time, one has to recognize that little progress has yet been made in putting into effect the more ambitious aim of comprehensive macroeconomic policy coordination endorsed at the Tokyo summit in 1986 and reaffirmed at the Venice summit in 1987. Even if the "blueprint" developed in this study is not in the event adopted for this purpose, we hope that its publication will contribute to the international search for an acceptable approach.

Our proposal is developed and presented in section 2. The study then proceeds to examine how the blueprint would have operated had it been in effect during the 1980s. Section 4 contrasts the proposal with alternative leading candidates for international monetary reform. Section 5 replies to various criticisms of the target zone proposal. The concluding section discusses some of the issues that arise in deciding whether to move on from the unpublished reference ranges of the Louvre accord to the formal system of policy coordination embodied in our blueprint.

2   The Blueprint

We start the explanation of our proposals by outlining the policy targets that a system of international macroeconomic policy coordination should promote.

Policy Targets

We take the primary objective of international macroeconomic policy coordination to be the achievement of as high a level and rate of growth of output in the participating countries, and indeed the world as a whole, as is possible on a sustained basis. The requirement of sustainability implies a need for the effective control of inflation and the avoidance of other financial disequilibria such as excessive deficits and surpluses in the balance of payments or the budget. Policy coordination should help each country to achieve these objectives by prescribing rules that are both helpful to itself and ensure that when its major partners follow similar rules the result is a set of mutually consistent policies.

Economists usually summarize these policy targets as rapid growth, low inflation, high employment, and an appropriate balance of payments on current account. The first three of these all relate to the state of the internal economy and are closely interdependent, especially in the short run. Not only does unemployment fall as output rises, and vice versa, but increases in output (relative to capacity) tend ceteris paribus to increase the rate of inflation (the Phillips curve relationship). It may nevertheless make sense to treat all three as targets, provided that their interdependence is clearly recognized. One certainly needs to take account of both output and inflation in order to decide a sensible trade-off between them, and an unemployment target can also be useful as a guide to the output growth that will be feasible and needed in the medium term (Gordon 1985).

The final target variable, the balance of payments on current account, should be treated as a means rather than an end from a sufficiently long-run standpoint, since a current account surplus transfers savings (i.e., capital) for investment abroad, while a deficit brings in foreign savings to supplement domestic savings. Countries benefit if capital flows to the places where it can earn the highest rate of return, and ideally one should analyze what that criterion implies for the desirable pattern of payments imbalances. In medium-run and short-run policy discussion, however, it is usual to treat the current account as an objective.

Two points need to be made about this objective, apart from the fact that its choice should ultimately be guided by securing an efficient international redistribution of savings. The first is that the targets chosen by different countries need to be internationally consistent. The world is a closed economy in which (when the statistics are measured correctly, which unfortunately they are not) one country's surplus is another country's deficit. This is a case of the famous "$n - 1$ problem" of international monetary economics: in a world of n countries, there are only $(n - 1)$ degrees of freedom to choose balance of payments targets. Unless one country is prepared to adopt a passive policy and allow its balance of payments to be determined as a residual, a role that would be allotted to the United States under a dollar standard but that the United States nowadays shows no sign of being willing to accept, then it is essential that the major countries negotiate an understanding on a set of mutually consistent targets.[1]

The second point is that the targets selected by individual countries need to be consistent with their *internal* policies, notably their fiscal policies. An important question arises as to whether any system of international policy coordination should simply accept the structural fiscal deficits of the participating countries as data, and adjust current account targets to them, or whether structural budget policy is a legitimate part of what should be coordinated. For example, when in 1981 the United States adopted a tax cut that had the effect of increasing the structural budget deficit by several percent of GNP for the indefinite future, should its partners have simply acquiesced in a consequential increase in the target US current account deficit

---

1. James Meade (1987) has recently developed some interesting ideas on how the need for such an understanding could be avoided. The basic idea is that each country would target some "wealth" variable, such as its overall level of savings or budget deficit, and would then use monetary policy to pursue an exchange rate target that would itself be adjusted until its "wealth" objective was achieved. Suppose, for example, that country A started off with too low a level of savings or too high a budget deficit. It would then reduce its interest rate so as to depreciate its exchange rate. Maintaining "internal balance" would require a compensatory tightening of fiscal policy, which would raise savings and reduce the budget deficit. Meade shows that, if each country pursues such an objective, their policies will converge. Our own assessment is that this approach may well have a role to play in helping to achieve agreement on current account targets, a topic not pursued in any depth in this study, but that the adjustments involved in the sequence described above are so lengthy that they are unlikely in practice to avoid the need for agreed current account targets.

or would it have been proper for them to object? We take the view that, at least to the extent that the new debt path appeared unsustainable (and thus contrary to the long-term interests of the United States as well as its partners), it would have been proper for foreign governments to object.

Intermediate Targets

It would be a mistake for a system of policy coordination to be focused directly on trying to achieve simultaneously the targets of high growth, low inflation, high employment, and a satisfactory set of payments balances. One reason is that, even within a single country, those objectives are often mutually contradictory in the short run. This would make it too easy for a government to dismiss the indicator signals on any occasion that it did not like the message, for it is virtually always possible to find one objective that could be compromised by a policy change. One might recall, for example, how many governments, perhaps most conspicuously that of Britain, pumped up demand in 1972–73 because of the historically high level of unemployment, despite the overwhelming danger of a further acceleration of inflation.

A second reason for not targeting the final objectives of policy directly is that some variables respond to policy changes only with a long lag. For example, current account balances lag at least two or three years behind exchange rate changes, principally because of the J curve. This means that a policy of devaluing (revaluing) whenever the current account was too large (too small) would lead to overshooting of the exchange rate. It is quite possible that the degree of overshooting would increase systematically over time, i.e., that the system would be unstable.

Both problems can be circumvented, or at least diminished, by a judicious choice of intermediate targets. These are variables that have no normative significance in themselves, but which it can be helpful to target in order to achieve the ultimate targets in the longer term. For example, instead of targeting the current account, the exchange rate can be targeted at a level calculated to produce a satisfactory current account in the medium term (the "fundamental equilibrium exchange rate," or FEER, of Williamson 1985). This circumvents the danger of instability noted above and was indeed the basis of the target zone proposal.

Our present proposals retain the exchange rate as one of two intermediate targets. We suggest that the other should be the rate of growth of nominal domestic demand, for reasons explained below. We then return to elaborate on the construction of the exchange rate target.

A Target for the Growth in Domestic Demand

In a closed economy, the growth in demand (nominal expenditure) is the same as that in nominal income (money GNP). Several distinguished economists such as Brittan (1987, especially ch. 6), Gordon (1985), and Meade (1984), as well as the *Economist*, the Commission of the European Communities and the Organization for Economic Cooperation and Development (OECD), have been persistent advocates of treating the growth of nominal income as an intermediate target. Indeed, the British government has in recent years had a loose target for nominal income growth.

The basic argument is that a nominal income rule fulfills the same function as a money supply rule, providing a "nominal anchor" to prevent inflation from taking off and a guide to expectations, while avoiding the shocks to demand that come from variations in velocity (which have in recent years proved much larger than anticipated in the heyday of monetarism). A money supply rule was in its turn argued to be preferable to a rule of seeking to stabilize prices (on account of the long lags involved) or output (on account of the danger of inflation creeping up, as happened in the years when undiluted Keynesianism held sway). The latter advantage is retained by the nominal income target.

Both high growth and low inflation are important objectives, and each is influenced by aggregate demand. An objective formulated in terms of either one alone therefore risks unacceptable damage to the other. If one focuses solely on output, one risks an inflationary explosion on the model of the early 1970s. Or if one focuses solely on price stability, one risks accepting the upward march of unemployment experienced in Europe in the 1980s. It seems more sensible to take both into account.

If both inflation and growth are too high or too low, then a nominal income target will give the same advice as a price or output rule, namely to contract or expand demand respectively. When one is too high and the other too low, a nominal income target provides a simple rule of thumb for trading off one against the other rather than simply ignoring either. And the rule also has the educational advantage of helping to make it clear that bigger wage increases, with their corollary of faster inflation, reduce the scope for real output growth.

The one disadvantage of a nominal income target in comparison to a money supply target is the longer lag before data become available. This lag is as long as that needed to obtain data on price or output developments.[2] The effects of this lag can be tempered by forecasting the development of nominal income, rather than just looking at last year's (or last quarter's) growth in nominal income when deciding whether a tightening or relaxation of policy is called for. There is in fact evidence that the International Monetary Fund (IMF) is rather better at forecasting the growth of nominal income than it is at forecasting either inflation or growth separately (Kenen, forthcoming), which is reassuring in this context.

We propose going beyond the conventional form of a nominal income target in two ways. The first is to allow the target to vary systematically with the state of the economy (or "endogenize" it). Gordon (1985) has already argued the case for a target path that is variable over time, rather than seeking a constant growth rate of nominal income of, say, 6 percent a year for the indefinite future. He shows that, for example, it is necessary gradually to decelerate the rate of growth of nominal income as the economy approaches full employment in order to achieve a "soft landing." Even apart from this dynamic consideration, it would obviously make little sense to put a permanent floor of 3 percent to the rate of inflation, as a 6 percent growth of nominal income would in a country with a 3 percent trend rate of real growth.

However, even Gordon's approach strikes us as overoptimistic in supposing that one can choose, once-and-for-all, a future path for nominal income. This poses two dangers if, for example, nominal income strays substantially above the planned path. One is that the public will not find promises to reduce nominal income back to its intended path to be credible. The other is that decisive action to bring it back will produce the sort of "crash landing" that the nonconstant path was intended to avert.

For these reasons, we propose a target that varies with the state of the economy. To understand the principles that should guide the choice of this target, consider first the case where the economy starts off "in equilibrium,"

---

2. The lag between policy action and changes in nominal income is nonetheless less than the lag between policy action and changes in inflation, since most of the initial impact of changes in aggregate demand tends to fall on output.

at an acceptably low rate of inflation and with unemployment at the NAIRU.[3] Then clearly the desirable rate of nominal income growth is simply the inherited inflation rate plus the growth rate of potential output. If inflation is acceptable but unemployment is above the NAIRU, one needs to add another term to provide for faster real output growth until the deflationary gap is closed. To secure a "soft landing," this extra output growth should tail off gradually as the deflationary gap diminishes.

Matters are somewhat more complex if inflation starts off above an acceptable level. If it is accepted that inflation cannot be brought to a standstill overnight, one will wish to expand demand so as to accommodate a *part* of the inherited inflation in the short run. But since inflation does indeed have to be reduced over time, unemployment must be pushed up to a level sufficient to achieve a decline in the inflation rate. Thus, the formula for nominal income growth has to allow also a fraction of the inherited rate of inflation and a deduction from real output growth calculated to produce an appropriate deflationary gap.

Two other points about a nominal income target are worth noting. One is that, provided that the target allows for only *partial* accommodation of past inflation, no threat is posed to the role of a nominal income target in providing a nominal anchor to control inflation.[4] The other is that at times governments will—and indeed should—try to use incomes and labor-market policies to reduce the unemployment cost of disinflation. It is important that they be realistic about what such policies can achieve: a nominal income target provides an excellent discipline, since failure of the policy to live up to expectations then implies that the extra inflation will be paid for with higher unemployment.

Our second amendment to the traditional proposal for seeking a constant rate of growth of nominal income involves replacing a target for the growth in *income* by one for the growth in *domestic demand*. The difference between the two concepts is equal to the change in (the domestic currency value of) the current account balance. A country, like the United States in 1987, that is aiming to improve its current account needs to make room for that

---

3. The "nonaccelerating inflation rate of unemployment."
4. Actually, an endogenous nominal income target like ours permits base drift and thus does not tie down the price *level*. It involves instead a (Wicksellian) attempt to tie down the *rate of inflation*. In technical terms it ensures that the inflation rate, but not the price level, has a finite asymptotic variance: see appendix B.

improvement by restraining the growth in domestic demand to less than its desired rate of growth in nominal income. Conversely, a country with an excessively large surplus (like Japan in 1987) needs to expand domestic demand by more than its nominal income should grow. The cause of international coordination could be powerfully aided by making explicit the obligations of countries with serious external imbalances to expand or contract their domestic demand by enough to accommodate the agreed adjustment process.[5]

A formula incorporating the principles developed above is presented in appendix A. This appendix also suggests parameter values that might have been appropriate for the G-7 countries in the 1980s, and develops the illustrative target values used in section 3.

The Target Exchange Rate

It has already been suggested that the exchange rate provides a good candidate for an intermediate target. This is because the exchange rate is the central determinant of the division of demand between domestic and foreign sources, and of supply between domestic and foreign markets: given that in the medium run one expects output to average close to full capacity, it is thus the central determinant of the current account. Hence to have a target for the current account implies a target for the exchange rate. This must be a target for the real effective exchange rate, rather than a target for the nominal rate or the bilateral rate against another currency, since it is the real effective exchange rate that is relevant to competitiveness and thus the balance of payments.

The principles that should guide choice of a target for the real effective exchange rate were laid out in Williamson (1985). The target is there described as the fundamental equilibrium exchange rate (FEER), and defined as the rate "which is expected to generate a current account surplus or deficit equal to the underlying capital flow over the cycle, given that the country is

---

5. Gordon (1985) has suggested another amendment to the proposal for targeting a constant rate of growth of nominal income. He proposes replacing nominal income by total final sales, thus excluding inventory changes on the ground that they are too transitory to be forecast or controlled. This difference is not material at the level of generality we are discussing, but merits consideration in any attempt to apply our proposals.

pursuing "internal balance" as best it can and not restricting trade for balance of payments reasons" (p. 14). To estimate a FEER, one needs to estimate the underlying or normal capital flow to which the current account should adjust,[6] as well as the "internal balance" targets which it, and its partners, can be expected to achieve and sustain in the medium term. One then has to use some model to estimate what real effective exchange rate would be needed to generate the target current account balance, given the levels of output to be expected, in the medium term.[7]

For operational purposes one has to translate a target for the *real* exchange rate into one for the *nominal* exchange rate. The implication of having a target specified in real terms is that as new statistics on differential inflation become available one would automatically make whatever adjustments in the nominal targets were needed to keep the real targets unchanged. Since data on price movements are published monthly, individual changes in the nominal target zones will be modest. Thus, nominal zones would crawl over time to maintain the real zones constant.

The policies that should be used to pursue the exchange rate target are discussed below, but essentially involve monetary policy. Before leaving this subject, however, one other topic needs to be addressed, namely why (or whether) an exchange rate target should be surrounded by a "zone" of acceptable rates, as envisaged in the target zone proposal. After all, it was not suggested above that the target for the growth in domestic demand should be surrounded by any zone, so it might be asked why the exchange rate target should need one.

The answer is in fact technical. Because domestic demand cannot be controlled precisely, due to lags and the indirect character of the policies available to influence it, in practice the outcome will differ from the target whether or not it is surrounded by a formal zone. The authorities will need to worry if these divergences are 4 percent or 5 percent but perhaps not if they are only 1 percent or 2 percent, but no useful information would be conveyed to the private sector by stating that the target is surrounded by a zone of ±3 percent, or some other number.

---

6. The need for these normal capital flows, which equal the current account targets, to be consistent both internationally and with domestic fiscal policy was noted above. The problem of selecting these targets is discussed again in section 5.

7. Such estimates were made for the Group of Five (G-5) currencies in Williamson (1985), and for the Canadian dollar in Williamson's appendix to Wonnacott (1987).

The situation is quite different with regard to exchange rates. Data are available by the minute, indeed by the second. The authorities can achieve an exchange rate target to any degree of accuracy they desire by taking sufficiently forceful action (unsterilized intervention). The idea of having a zone is to avoid having monetary policy buffeted by every shock in the foreign exchange market and to ensure that policy need react only when the consequence of inaction is serious (misalignment).

The target zone proposal as advanced by Williamson (1985) envisaged that zones might be quite wide, as much as ±10 percent. These wide limits were justified partly on the basis of the need to allow monetary policy to continue to play a significant role in domestic stabilization and partly because of skepticism as to our ability to calculate sensible exchange rate targets with any greater degree of accuracy. Once exchange rates have settled down from the enormous swings of recent years so that it is possible to get a better fix on where they need to be to achieve satisfactory payments outcomes, it may well make sense to envisage rather narrower bands (perhaps ±5 percent).

Williamson (1985) also suggested that target zones might have ''soft buffers,'' in the sense that a country would not have an absolute obligation to prevent rates from straying outside the zone under strong market pressure while it debated with its partners whether circumstances had changed in a way that justified a change in the zones or whether policies should be changed to push rates back into the zone. Two circumstances might justify bringing the soft buffers into play. One is where the balance of payments outlook changes suddenly and dramatically (oil price changes, for example). The other is where a country finds itself politically unable to take other measures (for example, on fiscal policy) to complement the monetary measures that would be needed to defend the target zone. Since the latter situation would not arise under the comprehensive proposals being developed here and the former seems unlikely (certainly with zones of ±10 percent), soft buffers might prove unnecessary.

In summary, our proposal involves one intermediate target related to the overall *level* of demand, and another (for the real exchange rate) that governs the medium-run *composition* of demand (and division of supply) between external and internal sources (destinations).[8] Between them, these two will

---

8. Thus, we are suggesting one intermediate target for what Harry Johnson (1958) termed ''expenditure-switching policies'' and another for what he termed ''expenditure-reducing policies,'' which may more generally be described as ''expenditure-changing policies.''

determine both the level of income and the current account. Together with those forces that govern the price-output breakdown of income, including labor-market and incomes policies as well as the supply side, the level of income governs both inflation and growth, and thereby in turn also unemployment. Hence control of the two suggested intermediate targets governs the evolution of all the final targets identified above.

The Assignment Problem

The question of "assignment" refers to the principles that should be adopted in order to relate policy instruments to targets. In the present instance we have reduced the targets to two intermediate targets in the case of each of the n participating countries, one for the growth in its (nominal) domestic demand and one for its real effective exchange rate. Each country has two broad policy instruments, fiscal policy and monetary policy, with which to pursue these two objectives. How should those policies be assigned in order to pursue the $2n$ intermediate targets?

Before answering this question, it is necessary to spell out our choice of monetary and fiscal instruments. Monetary policy can be interpreted *either* as the rate of growth of a monetary aggregate, *or* as the level of (short-term) interest rates, but these are not independent instruments. Neither are they equivalent instruments: they imply different reactions to exogenous shocks.[9]

We favor a monetary policy that focuses on control over the level of short-term interest rates. This is the way most central banks operate: those that still try to target monetary aggregates raise short-term interest rates when their chosen aggregate rises too fast. It is much more useful if policy rules can be specified directly in terms of what is actually used as a policy instrument. Furthermore, the intellectual argument that led most economists in the 1970s to prefer a monetary aggregate as a measure of monetary policy, namely the asserted stability of the relationship between spending and money versus the slippage of the relationship between spending and interest rates as inflation changes, is unpersuasive today. Velocity (the relationship between spending and money) has proved to be highly variable, while it is possible

---

9. In terms of the familiar IS/LM analysis, a policy of controlling the interest rate leads to a horizontal LM curve and a policy of controlling the money supply to the usual upwardly sloping LM curve, which imply different reactions to anything that shifts the IS curve.

to have a shot at measuring real interest rates even ex ante, and thus make at least rough correction for the slippage of the relation between money and interest rates.[10]

We do not make a similar attempt to specify whether changes in fiscal policy should take the form of changes in tax rates or in expenditures. This is a topic that is surely within the area of legitimate national discretion, for the differences in the balance of payments effects of different policy choices with a similar fiscal impulse are second order. In making their choices on this issue some countries may be influenced by the fear that tax increases will have a perverse effect on nominal income for a considerable period (Meade 1987). Since expenditure changes are difficult to implement quickly, this may well imply that it is unrealistic to believe that fiscal policy can be used for "fine tuning." (This is the principal reason for believing that target zones will probably have to be quite wide.)

---

10. The difference between adopting nominal income rather than the money supply as an intermediate target when the interest rate is used as the monetary instrument is modest. A money supply target involves inverting the money demand function and setting the interest rate i to secure

$$i = (kq + p - m^* + \epsilon)/\lambda,$$

where k is the income elasticity of demand for money, q is output, p is the price level, m^* is the target money supply, ϵ is the stochastic shock to the demand for money function, and λ is the interest elasticity of demand for money. Pursuing a nominal income target y^* by adjusting the interest rate in proportion to the deviation from target implies

$$i = \gamma(q + p - y^*).$$

How does this compare with the money supply rule? Clearly there is a change of target, and q and p are now weighted equally. In addition the rule is now more flexible and less subject to "velocity" shocks. Thus the coefficient γ which measures the proportional response can, but need not necessarily, be set equal to λ^{-1}, the inverse of the (semi) interest elasticity of demand for money: policymakers can choose γ as they judge fit. It is perhaps unexplained and persistent variations in the velocity of money (here captured by ϵ) which have given policymakers the greatest concern in pursuing money supply targets; but, as is evident from the formula, ϵ is absent from the nominal income formulation. (Implicitly, this means that such unexplained fluctuations in velocity will be accommodated, as interest rates are geared solely to movements of output and prices.)

The response of policymakers may, of course, be more complicated than the simple proportional response discussed above. In particular they may also respond to the *integral* of such deviations, see Edison, Miller, and Williamson (1987). But the basic point, that responding to nominal income permits flexibility and avoids varying interest rates every time velocity shifts, remains true.

The problem is therefore that of managing interest rates and fiscal policy in each country with a view to achieving the intermediate targets for a set of growth rates of nominal domestic demand and (mutually consistent) real effective exchange rates.

One principle is suggested immediately by the monetary approach to the balance of payments, whose valid central theorem points to the close dependence of the exchange rate on the supply of money. It is therefore entirely natural to expect a rise in (real) interest rates to strengthen a currency, since it increases the return to holding that currency. Thus, our rule (B), in the box on page 2, states that a country whose currency is too weak (strong) relative to its target should be expected to raise (lower) its (real) interest rate. This rule should be supplemented, or at times might even be replaced, by the use of intervention in the foreign exchange markets, but sterilized intervention is too weak an instrument to be relied on exclusively for exchange rate management given the need to establish credibility with the market.

While such a rule would govern the *relative* interest rates among currencies, it would not tie down the *average* level of interest rates in the world as a whole. This is another manifestation of the "$n - 1$ problem": since n currencies have only $n - 1$ exchange rates, they can be controlled through the $n - 1$ interest rate *differentials*. The *average world interest rate* provides an extra degree of freedom that should be determined according to other principles.

The mark of a symmetrical world system is that a "world variable" such as the average world short-term interest rate should be determined by the needs of the world economy as a whole rather than those of a particular country (as under a dollar standard). The natural application of this principle in the present context involves raising the world level of short-term interest rates when the world is in a dangerously strong boom and lowering it during a recession. (The problem of ensuring that these *variations* in the level of world interest rates take place around a suitable *average* is addressed subsequently.) And the natural interpretation of whether the world economy is growing too fast or too slow is to ask whether the *aggregate* nominal demand of the participants is growing faster or slower than the *sum* of their targets.[11]

---

11. One reason for preferring the G-7 over narrower groupings like the G-3 or G-5 as the unit for policy coordination is that it embraces substantially over 50 percent of gross world product, and thus minimizes the danger that the situation of the group whose needs determine global policies will differ from that of the world as a whole.

FIGURE 1   **Guidelines for adjusting interest rates**

		Growth of world demand		
		Weak	On target	Strong
Exchange rate	Weak	No change	+	+ +
	On target	−	No change	+
	Strong	− −	−	No change

Together, these two rules would provide fairly specific advice to central banks to guide their monetary policies. The guidelines are summarized in figure 1, where a positive sign suggests that interest rates should be increased and a double positive that they should be increased sharply. Of course, such rules should not be applied mechanically. A country whose own demand was growing more slowly than desired even though world demand was on target might prefer to avoid raising interest rates even if its own currency was weak. This would be the sort of case in which a country could be expected to resort to sterilized intervention: provided the market believes that sterilized intervention would be backed up by stronger measures (interest rate increases) if the need arose, it might well be effective. Alternatively, such a country might allow its currency to depreciate within the zone.[12]

Nevertheless, situations could clearly arise in which the rules for interest rate policy laid out above would run counter to the needs of the domestic economy, and in particular to the need to expand or restrain demand in order to counter recession or inflation (respectively). It is in such situations that a third assignment rule, governing short-run fiscal policy, would come into play. An excessively weak growth in domestic demand in circumstances in which interest rates were constant or rising would create a case for fiscal expansion (tax cuts or expenditure increases). Conversely, excessively strong demand growth in circumstances where interest rates should be cut to keep the exchange rate within bounds, such as 1983–84 in the United States, would call for increased fiscal discipline.

None of the assignment rules suggested here is intended to imply that governments should react slavishly to past changes in nominal demand. Statistics on income and expenditure become available only with a substantial

---

12. This is one of the reasons for suggesting that target zones for exchange rates should be wide. See McKinnon (1971) for the underlying theory.

lag, so that there would be serious dangers in pushing world interest rates down just because the latest statistics showed a below-target growth in world nominal demand: such a policy could lead to a building of liquidity that could fuel a new bout of inflation. Rather, the authorities should look ahead as best they can, and nudge interest rates down when the outlook appears depressed and the inflationary dangers minimal. A good test of whether monetary expansion is safe is whether long-term rates also move down following a cut in short-term rates.

Our suggested set of assignment rules can be summarized as follows:

(A) The *average level* of world (real) short-term interest rates should be revised up (down) if aggregate growth of nominal income is threatening to exceed (fall short of) the sum of the target growth of nominal demand for the participating countries.

(B) *Differences* in short-term interest rates among countries should be revised when necessary to supplement intervention in the exchange markets to prevent the deviation of currencies from their target ranges.

(C) National *fiscal policies* should be revised with a view to achieving national target rates of growth of domestic demand.

Medium-Term Constraints

The rules set out above are essentially rules for short-run or anticyclical management of the world economy. They need to be supplemented by at least two criteria relating to the medium run.

One of these relates to the world level of interest rates. If the system started off with a historically high level of interest rates caused by a mix of expansionary fiscal and contractionary monetary policy, the rules (A) to (C) could perpetuate this situation. Yet fundamentally the interest rate should be set at a level that optimizes intertemporal resource allocation. This is not inconsistent with the anticyclical pattern proposed by rule (A), since in a recession the opportunity cost of current spending diminishes and hence the incentive effect of lower interest rates in increasing current expenditure is appropriate.

However, one also requires that the interest rate *fluctuate around* a level that produces appropriate incentives to save and invest for the future and avoid a situation in which current expenditure has to be propped up by an excessive level of deficit spending by government. A real interest rate above its historically normal range (2 percent to 3 percent) for a sustained period should therefore be taken as prima facie evidence of a need for a joint medium-run effort to tighten fiscal policy. A real interest rate below that range for a sustained period seems more likely to indicate excessively loose monetary policy than excessively tight fiscal policy. In either event, the participating countries should adjust the *mix* of fiscal and monetary policy.

A second medium-run issue concerns fiscal discipline. Much concern arose in Europe and Japan in the late 1970s that expansionary fiscal policies intended to expand demand were leading the state to insolvency. Programs of fiscal consolidation were therefore given priority over short-run demand management, especially in Germany, Japan, and the United Kingdom.

Indeed, under some circumstances fiscal expansion may even prove counterproductive from the standpoint of supporting aggregate demand. This is not to endorse the standpoint of those German spokesmen who sound as if they believe that an increased fiscal deficit will inevitably erode confidence to the point where demand will fall rather than rise.[13] But however implausible this argument may be in the context of low budget deficit, low public-sector debt, low inflation, and low capacity utilization in 1987 Germany, it is quite likely that it holds true under less favorable circumstances. Where it might hold true, it would be prudent to suspend the rule that fiscal policy should be expansionary when nominal demand grows undesirably slowly. Under such circumstances priority would need to be given to fiscal consolidation. It is an alarming thought that such a situation could arise in the United States if a crisis of confidence caused a collapse of the dollar before the budget deficit is brought under control.[14]

An agreement on the danger point at which fiscal consolidation should take precedence over the maintenance of demand might be worthwhile. The basic principle would be that fiscal consolidation would have priority when existing policies threaten an explosive growth of the public debt, but not when the debt-to-GNP ratio is declining or set to level out at a reasonable figure. As shown by Marris (1987, pp. 180–89), such assessments require taking account of two variables, the debt-to-GNP ratio and the structural

---

13. They are not claiming that an increased fiscal deficit is likely to cause some crowding out of other expenditures (which is of course likely, at least if the money supply rather than the interest rate is maintained constant), but seem to argue that crowding out will be more than 100 percent.

14. This is the scenario laid out by Stephen Marris (1985).

budget balance (strictly, the "mid-cycle primary budget position as a percentage of GNP").

Doubtless other cases might arise in which rules (A) to (C) would need to be overridden. Any system of policy coordination will need to be flexible enough to allow for derogation from the normal rules when circumstances warrant. Ideally, such derogations should be rare exceptions that are allowed only for good cause after a searching examination in some appropriate international forum like the G-7 or the IMF. Whether the need for derogation will be rare depends on whether the rules are "robust," i.e., remain appropriate under a wide range of circumstances. Although we believe that our rules are indeed robust, for reasons explained in appendix B, derogation procedures would doubtless have to be lax until the system had been in operation for some time and proved its worth.

3   The Indicators in Practice, 1980–87

Any far-reaching proposal for economic reform should be accompanied by an examination of the probable impact that the reform would have had if it had been operational in the past. Accordingly, the present section examines how our blueprint could have been expected to influence the economic history of the 1980s.

A first effort in this direction was undertaken in a paper by the present authors in association with Hali Edison (Edison, Miller, and Williamson 1987). This involved a simulation of one of the large multicountry macroeconometric models, the US Federal Reserve Board's MCM (multicountry model), from 1976 to 1985. The relevant part of that study is reproduced as appendix C.

That simulation does not incorporate the full set of rules developed in this study: in particular, it does not include the domestic demand targets. In fact, the first simulation included only rule (B), for adjusting national interest rates to limit the deviation of the exchange rate from a target level. A second simulation added a compensatory fiscal policy designed to keep output equal to its baseline level. The key results suggested by these simulations were:

• A system of adjusting interest rates so as to limit the deviation of exchange rates from consistent target values would have been quite effective in reducing misalignments without requiring vast changes in interest rates. (For example, the appreciation of the dollar over the period 1980–85 would have been almost halved, from over 65 percent to under 35 percent.) This is true even though no allowance was made for sterilized intervention or the guidance provided to markets by the publication of target zones.

• The interest rate adjustments required to limit the rise of the dollar in 1983–85 would not have aborted the deceleration of inflation achieved in the United States, at least within the time period of the study. This favorable experience does, however, owe something to the restraining effects of higher interest rates and a higher dollar in 1979–80 which the rules would have produced.

• The better alignment of exchange rates would not have reduced payments imbalances greatly, at least in the short run, unless it had been reinforced by compensatory fiscal policy.

• The interest rate adjustments required to limit misalignments could have had perverse cyclical effects, notably in deepening the 1982–83 recessions in Canada and Germany, unless their domestic effects had been countered by a compensatory fiscal policy.

The crucial importance of a compensatory fiscal policy revealed by these results was one factor that led us to the domestic demand rule. A second factor was recognition that while changes in government expenditure that froze output to its level in the baseline, the form of compensatory fiscal policy used in the simulation, may be simple to implement in an econometric model, they are neither feasible nor desirable in the real world.

Another way of gaining some feeling as to how our proposal might have worked is to examine the policy pressures to which governments would have been subjected over the years by the indicator system. In appendix A we calculate what our proposed demand growth targets might have been for the G-7 countries (United States, Japan, Germany, France, Italy, Britain, and Canada), given that history up to the year in question was what it historically was. The discussion of each country below, based on those figures plus a comparison of exchange rates with the FEERs estimated in Williamson (1985), thus differs from the simulation briefly reported above in that those simulations took account of the impact of policy changes in preceding years on the situation in any particular year.

United States

The United States, like the other G-7 countries, entered the 1980s with a high rate of inflation inherited from the 1970s that was being aggravated by the second oil price shock and by a weak dollar, which in 1980 lay between 5 percent and 10 percent below its estimated FEER.[15] The inflation had prompted the adoption of a "monetarist" policy change by the Federal Reserve Board in late 1979, leading to high interest rates and a near-recession in early 1980. Policy was relaxed quickly and the economy was recovering by 1981, when the Reagan tax reductions were approved by Congress and the vista of limitless budget deficits opened up. One result was much higher interest rates, bringing on a sharp recession in 1982. This caused both a major decline in inflation and the Third World debt crisis.

Recovery from recession in 1983 and catch-up growth in 1984 were accompanied by a further strengthening of the already overvalued dollar, which combined to create a vast current account deficit that climbed to $141 billion by 1986. The dollar peaked in early 1985 and by 1987 had fallen back to near the Williamson estimate of its FEER,[16] though without as yet a major improvement in the current account in value terms. Meanwhile, the economy has expanded roughly in line with capacity, with a modest level of slack and an inflation rate that is still distinctly positive though much lower than in the previous decade.

---

15. FEER estimates are taken from the work of Williamson (1985) and Williamson in Wonnacott (1987). A very rough idea of the relationship of five of the G-7 exchange rates to their target zones can also be gained from figure C.1 of the present volume. However, those figures are based on an effective exchange rate defined only in terms of the four other currencies shown in that figure. The error thus introduced is particularly important for Germany, whose effective exchange rate is in the real world stabilized much more than in figure C.1 through its stable relationship to the other currencies in the European Monetary System.

16. It should be recalled that the definition of the FEER assumes "internal balance" both at home and abroad. Since fiscal policies have not been adjusted adequately to support reestablishment of internal balance either in the United States or Europe (or perhaps Japan), an estimate that the dollar is near its FEER is not tantamount to a prediction that the US current account deficit will subside to a sustainable level without further policy changes.

Figures 2 and 3 (see also tables 1 and 2) reveal that the actual growth in US demand in 1980 was somewhat (2.5 percentage points) less than the target growth rate calculated according to the formula suggested in appendix A, while aggregate G-7 demand grew at almost exactly the target rate. Policy was generally restrictive, especially in the United States early in the year, when interest rates reached very high levels. Such a restrictive stance was needed in view of the inflationary pressures and the absence of substantial excess capacity, even if it was overdone (according to our formula) in the United States.

Both the United States and the G-7 experienced some recovery in growth in 1981 following the policy relaxation in 1980. Aggregate demand growth was modestly above target in the G-7 and substantially greater in the United States, with inflation falling only slightly in the G-7 and actually rising further in the United States, suggesting that the relaxation of 1980 was premature or excessive. A more modest relaxation in monetary policy would have been preferable (monetary rather than fiscal policy being the indicated candidate both because of the excessive growth of G-7 nominal income and the weakness of the dollar in 1980).

The dollar passed its FEER early in 1981 and by the end of the year was already around where the top of a 10 percent target zone would have been, pulled up by the high interest rates resulting from larger expected budget deficits. These facts suggest that fiscal policy was already too expansionary, or expected to become too expansionary, before the end of 1981.

If demand grew somewhat too fast in 1981, the same can certainly not be said of 1982, the year of the sharpest postwar recession. Actual demand growth fell substantially short of that called for by our suggested formula, in the G-7 and even more in the United States. The excessive strength of the dollar and the generality of the recession would both have pointed to a monetary relaxation as appropriate—a move that was in fact initiated in mid-1982, perhaps partly in response to the emergence of the debt crisis. A demand growth target might have pointed to the need for this decline in interest rates somewhat sooner than it actually occurred: policy reactions were delayed by the then-prevalent fixation on monetary targets, which were giving misleading signals because of the decline in velocity. A quicker fall in interest rates would have tempered the recession and attenuated the debt crisis. Nevertheless, we are not claiming that a better intermediate target would have avoided the recession, which took a long time to be recognized and was simply unforeseen at the beginning of the year (Gordon 1985).

The recession did at least produce a big decline in inflation, which tended

FIGURE 2   **Group of Seven: actual and target rates of growth in domestic demand**

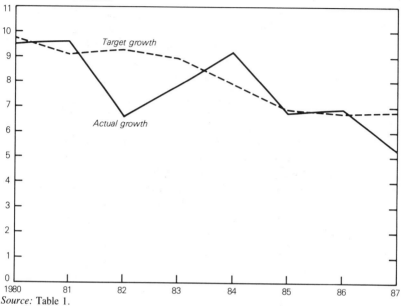

Source: Table 1.

TABLE 1   **Group of Seven: target demand change and actual outcomes, 1980–87** (percentage increase)

Year	Target demand growth $\hat{y}^*$	Actual demand growth $\hat{y}$	Actual increase in nominal income	Increase in GNP g	Increase in GNP deflator $\hat{p}$
1980	9.7	9.5	10.6	1.0	9.5
1981	9.1	9.6	10.4	1.5	8.8
1982	9.3	6.6	6.3	−0.6	6.9
1983	9.0	7.8	7.5	2.7	4.7
1984	7.9	9.2	8.8	4.7	3.9
1985	6.9	6.8	6.8	3.0	3.7
1986	6.7	6.9	5.8	2.4	3.3
1987	6.8	5.2[a]	5.2[a]	2.3[a]	2.9[a]

Note: Weights based on 1980 GNP converted at market exchange rates.
Source: Column 1, tables A.1–A.7; columns 2–5, *OECD Economic Outlook* data base.
a. Estimate from June 1987 *OECD Economic Outlook*.

to reduce the target for growth in domestic demand. In fact, the pickup in demand growth in the United States was in line with our target in 1983, although it remained somewhat below our target in the G-7. The already excessive and further increasing strength of the dollar, coupled with the weakness of G-7 growth, would have pointed to a cut in interest rates, although a substantial reduction would have required a compensatory tightening of fiscal policy to keep nominal income on track.

By 1984 actual demand growth was running ahead of our target, by a modest margin in the G-7 as a whole but a massive 5 percent in the United States. Since the dollar continued to head further above its target zone throughout the year, the rules would have called for major policy changes in the United States involving both lower interest rates to reduce the value of the dollar and a major tightening of fiscal policy to reduce the growth of domestic demand. In retrospect it seems even more clear than it did at the time that this would have been the best chance for a (macroeconomically) painless cut in the US fiscal deficit.

By 1985 inflation was at last getting down toward tolerable levels, both in the G-7 and the United States, and growth was maintained. The dollar's rise was finally reversed. Demand grew at a rate close to our target. Since the dollar remained vastly overvalued, however, our indicators would have suggested the desirability of a different fiscal-monetary mix, with lower interest rates and a lower budget deficit. The situation remained broadly unchanged in 1986, except that the dollar had fallen back to near the top of its target zone by the end of the year. Our indicators suggest that domestic demand is growing at an appropriate rate in the United States in 1987, but significantly slower than is desirable in the G-7 as a whole.

In our judgment the recommendations that would have been generated by the proposed indicators could have been expected to lead to better economic performance. They would have called for a more even pattern of demand growth at the beginning of the period when policy produced a near-recession followed by the 1981 rebound and to a quicker relaxation of monetary policy in the 1982 recession, which seem appropriate recommendations even if they would not have been able to fine tune away the recession. And they would have pointed to a markedly different mix of fiscal and monetary policy in later years, which would have limited the overvaluation of the dollar. It is no great surprise that the indicators should have produced these results: they were designed to do so.

Some might nevertheless question whether such policy changes would

FIGURE 3   **United States: actual and target rates of growth in domestic demand**

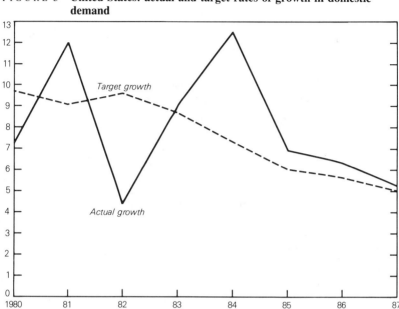

Source: Table 2.

TABLE 2   **United States: target demand change and actual outcomes, 1980–87** (percentage increase)

Year	Target demand growth $\hat{y}^*$	Actual demand growth $\hat{y}$	Actual increase in nominal income	Increase in GNP g	Increase in GNP deflator $\hat{p}$
1980	9.7	7.2	8.9	−0.2	9.0
1981	9.1	12.0	11.7	1.8	9.7
1982	9.6	4.4	3.7	−2.5	6.4
1983	8.7	9.0	7.6	3.6	3.9
1984	7.3	12.5	10.6	6.5	3.9
1985	6.0	6.9	6.2	2.8	3.3
1986	5.6	6.3	5.2	2.5	2.7
1987	5.0	5.2[a]	6.0[a]	2.5[a]	3.4[a]

Source: Column 1, table A.1; columns 2–5, *OECD Economic Outlook* data base.
a. Estimate from June 1987 *OECD Economic Outlook*.

have been helpful. For example, the question might be raised as to whether a recession of the severity of 1982 was not the necessary price for squeezing inflation back down to acceptable levels. We are not aware of any evidence for believing that sharp recessions have disproportionate effects in reducing inflation and actually find the contention rather implausible,[17] but the point is of sufficiently fundamental importance that it needs to be analyzed carefully before making any final commitment to an indicator system that would preclude similar squeezes in the future.

Japan

Japan started the 1980s with the lowest rate of inflation of any of the major industrial countries. It maintained the fastest rate of growth of any of them, an average of over 4 percent per year over 1980–85, and largely avoided the recession of the early 1980s. Only in 1986, under the impact of a violently appreciating yen, did growth fall below 3 percent. Until then, however, growth was strongly sustained by external demand, leading to a massive $86 billion current account surplus (over 5 percent of GNP) by 1986. It is noteworthy that Japan achieved its strong growth with the lowest rate of inflation among the G-7, and has now enjoyed six consecutive years of virtual price stability. It did this despite a yen that was consistently weak, being near or below the bottom edge of its hypothetical target zone until well into 1986.

As can be seen from figure 4, actual growth in domestic demand has been consistently lower than our target rate ever since 1980. The more rapid demand growth called for by the indicator would surely have been helpful. In association with the stronger yen that would have resulted from lower interest rates in the United States not fully matched by declines in Japan, the faster growth in demand could have prevented the Japanese current account surplus from building up to its present excessive size without jeopardizing the impressive growth rate that the Japanese economy maintained until 1986 (table 3)—when its excessive surplus finally came home to roost. The shortfall in domestic demand growth was particularly dramatic in early 1987, and will

---

17. The original Phillips curve was convex to the origin, implying diminishing anti-inflation returns to an intensification of recessionary shocks. See Phillips (1958).

FIGURE 4   **Japan: actual and target rates of growth in domestic demand**

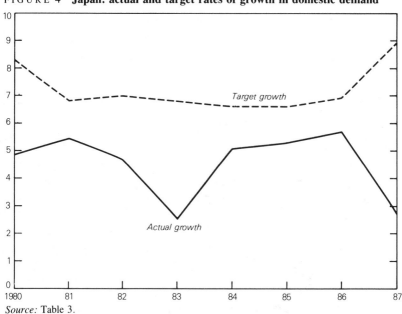

Source: Table 3.

TABLE 3   **Japan: target demand change and actual outcomes, 1980–87**
(percentage increase)

Year	Target demand growth $\hat{y}^*$	Actual demand growth $\hat{y}$	Actual increase in nominal income	Increase in GNP g	Increase in GNP deflator $\hat{p}$
1980	8.3	4.8	8.2	4.3	3.8
1981	6.8	5.5	7.0	3.7	3.2
1982	7.0	4.7	5.0	3.1	1.8
1983	6.8	2.5	4.0	3.2	0.8
1984	6.6	5.1	6.4	5.1	1.2
1985	6.6	5.3	6.3	4.7	1.5
1986	6.9	5.7	4.3	2.4	1.8
1987	8.9	2.7[a]	2.3[a]	2.1[a]	0.2[a]

Source: Column 1, table A.2; columns 2–5, *OECD Economic Outlook* data base.
a. Estimate from June 1987 *OECD Economic Outlook*.

remain large even if the ¥ 6 trillion expansion package announced in April (whose effects are not included in the estimates shown) were to add 2 percentage points or so to demand.

Germany

Like Japan, growth in domestic demand in Germany consistently fell short of our target value in the first half of the 1980s (figure 5). Like the Japanese yen, the deutsche mark spent most of the period from 1981 to 1986 near or below the bottom margin of its hypothetical target zone. And like Japan, Germany built up a large current account surplus ($36 billion in 1986) in the years of the strong dollar.

Economic performance, however, was substantially less satisfactory. Inflation as measured by the GNP deflator has dropped below 2 percent (and then marginally) only in 1987, compared to six consecutive years in Japan. And output growth has averaged a derisory 1.4 percent per year as compared to Japan's 3.8 percent, leading to a major rise in unemployment to over 8 percent. Although the average growth rate exceeded the assumed growth rate of capacity (2.5 percent per year) in 1984 (table 4), the excess was too modest and short-lived to have made a big dent in the deflationary gap. Germany is still awaiting a spurt of catch-up growth following the 1980–82 recession.

Domestic demand in Germany (and for that matter in Japan) would have been strengthened to some extent by the lower real interest rates that would have developed during and after the 1982 recession according to rule (A) and the lower US fiscal deficit. It is nevertheless reasonable to suppose that a serious attempt to meet the targets shown in figure 5 would have required a less hasty program of fiscal consolidation. Although the German government would certainly have disagreed at the time, and may still do so, we believe that faster demand expansion would in fact have been in Germany's best interests, in limiting the buildup of a wasteful deflationary gap as well as the development of payments imbalances. Had the lower interest rate differential in favor of the dollar also prevented serious undervaluation of the deutsche mark, a higher rate of growth might well have been combined with a lower rate of inflation. The preliminary data for 1987 suggest that the problem of deficient growth in German domestic demand remains unresolved.

FIGURE 5   **Germany: actual and target rates of growth in domestic demand**

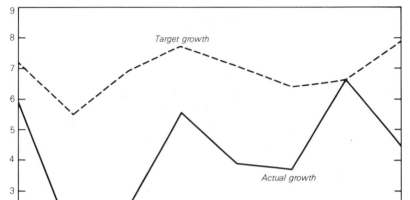

Source: Table 4.

TABLE 4   **Germany: target demand change and actual outcomes, 1980–87**
(percentage increase)

Year	Target demand growth $\hat{y}^*$	Actual demand growth $\hat{y}$	Actual increase in nominal income	Increase in GNP g	Increase in GNP deflator $\hat{p}$
1980	7.2	5.9	6.4	1.5	4.8
1981	5.5	1.4	4.0	0.0	4.0
1982	6.9	2.4	3.4	−1.0	4.4
1983	7.7	5.6	5.2	1.9	3.2
1984	7.1	3.9	5.0	2.9	2.0
1985	6.4	3.7	4.7	2.4	2.2
1986	6.6	6.6	5.5	2.3	3.1
1987	7.9	4.4[a]	3.2[a]	1.5[a]	1.7[a]

Source: Column 1, table A.3; columns 2–5, *OECD Economic Outlook* data base.
a. Estimate from June 1987 *OECD Economic Outlook.*

France

Actual growth in domestic demand substantially exceeded the target we calculate for France in 1980 (figure 6). Unlike other countries, the excess not only remained in 1981 but increased in 1982, a reflection of the initial expansionary thrust of the Mitterrand regime. Instead of falling in the worldwide recession year of 1982, French output rose by 1.8 percent (table 5), but at the cost of a further increase in inflation and a very substantial current account deficit. These developments led to a reversal of the policy of reflation, a reversal reputedly eased by the French desire to remain within the European Monetary System (EMS). The deflationary policy did indeed succeed in reducing both inflation and the current account deficit over the following years, although at the cost of a growth rate that has remained below the growth of capacity ever since. During this period the actual growth of domestic demand remained below our target rate until 1986, and the French franc remained weak but within its hypothetical target zone. (The latter is defined in effective terms and is therefore shielded from the appreciation of the dollar by the high proportion of French trade conducted with other European countries; the bilateral rate between the French franc and the US dollar became misaligned by vastly more than 10 percent.)

Our indicators would have cautioned against the initial ambitious reflation of 1981, and the higher world interest rates that rule (A) would have produced in 1981 would have helped restrain the growth in demand. From 1983 on, the demand growth indicator would have counseled a less severe policy of restraint than the one pursued, and the lower world interest rates produced by rule (A) would again have helped France achieve this objective. It is debatable whether the output gains from less severe restraint would have justified the delay in disinflation, although the latter would have been aided had the dollar been less overvalued. In 1987 France appears, like Germany, to be suffering from a substantial shortfall in domestic demand.

Italy

Italy started the period with a very high rate of inflation and buoyant growth, both fed by a massive 28 percent expansion in domestic demand in 1980. This was vastly above the rate that would have been counseled by our

FIGURE 6   **France: actual and target rates of growth in domestic demand**

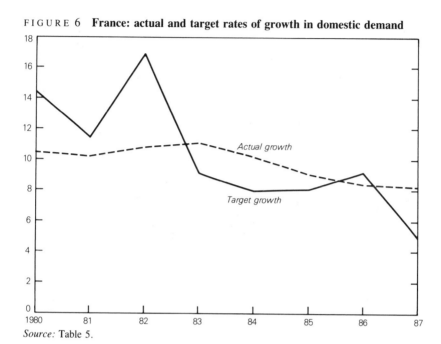

Source: Table 5.

TABLE 5   **France: target demand change and actual outcomes, 1980–87**
(percentage increase)

Year	Target demand growth $\hat{y}^*$	Actual demand growth $\hat{y}$	Actual increase in nominal income	Increase in GNP g	Increase in GNP deflator $\hat{p}$
1980	10.5	14.4	13.4	1.0	12.2
1981	10.2	11.4	12.3	0.5	11.8
1982	10.8	16.9	14.7	1.8	12.6
1983	11.1	9.1	10.3	0.7	9.5
1984	10.2	8.0	8.8	1.5	7.2
1985	9.1	9.2	7.3	1.4	5.8
1986	8.4	4.9	7.4	2.0	5.3
1987	8.2	4.7[a]	4.5[a]	1.0[a]	3.1[a]

Source: Column 1, table A.4; columns 2–5, *OECD Economic Outlook* data base.
a. Estimate from June 1987 *OECD Economic Outlook.*

formula, which would have continued to advise more restraint than that actually observed in 1981–82 (figure 7). In the years since 1983, when Italy achieved major success in disinflating (table 6), domestic demand growth was very close to our target.

Although Williamson (1985) did not make an estimate of the lira's FEER, subsequent calculations led him to conclude that the exchange rate of early 1987 was broadly appropriate. This would suggest that, like the French franc, the lira was undervalued for most of the period 1981–86, although once again the shield afforded by membership in the EMS limited the effective misalignment.

Unfortunately, the fact that Italy seems close to both of our intermediate targets in 1987 does not mean that all is as it should be. This is a case in which the fiscal situation is clearly unsatisfactory and unsustainable, with a debt-to-GNP ratio of over 100 percent and a fiscal deficit over 10 percent of GNP. Although Italy has a program for fiscal consolidation, the progress in that direction is painfully, perhaps dangerously, slow. This is a case in which the short-term rules perhaps ought to be overridden by the medium-term constraints.

United Kingdom

In 1980 British inflation was, as in Italy, around 20 percent, but in strong contrast output fell. Despite this, our demand growth indicator suggests that the growth in nominal demand in 1980 was excessive (figure 8). This was perhaps because of the peculiar mix of policies adopted by the Thatcher government after it first took office in 1979, combining a relaxed attitude to wage increases and a shift in the burden of taxation toward indirect taxes with strong monetary restraint.

In 1981–82 the growth in demand was less than the calculated target, with the discrepancy being particularly large in 1981, the year when 364 economists signed a letter to the London *Times* denouncing the deflationary budget. Our calculations thus suggest that their concern was well founded, whatever may be thought of the style of the letter. A major reason for the inadequate demand growth and severity of the resulting recession (table 7) was the tight monetary policy, which interacted with the high oil price and North Sea oil to produce a vast overvaluation of the pound sterling (Buiter and Miller 1981). Throughout the period under review, the pound was above its estimated

FIGURE 7 **Italy: actual and target rates of growth in domestic demand**

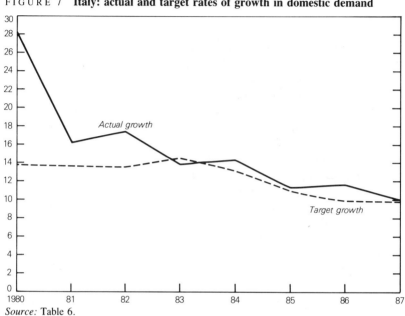

Source: Table 6.

TABLE 6 **Italy: target demand change and actual outcomes, 1980–87**
(percentage increase)

Year	Target demand growth $\hat{y}^*$	Actual demand growth $\hat{y}$	Actual increase in nominal income	Increase in GNP g	Increase in GNP deflator $\hat{p}$
1980	13.8	28.2	25.4	3.9	20.6
1981	13.6	16.2	18.6	0.2	18.3
1982	13.5	17.4	17.2	−0.5	17.8
1983	14.4	13.8	14.7	−0.2	14.9
1984	13.1	14.3	13.9	2.8	10.8
1985	10.9	11.3	11.3	2.3	8.8
1986	9.9	11.6	11.2	2.7	8.3
1987	9.7	10.0[a]	8.7[a]	2.9[a]	5.6[a]

Source: Column 1, table A.5; columns 2–5, *OECD Economic Outlook* data base.
a. Estimate from June 1987 *OECD Economic Outlook*.

FEER, and for most of the time—especially in 1980–81—well above its hypothetical target zone. Our indicators would thus have called for a markedly less restrictive monetary policy, which would have limited the destruction of British manufacturing industry that occurred at that time,[18] though presumably at the cost of somewhat delaying the reduction in inflation. (The simulations reported in appendix C suggest that this delay would have been modest had overall demand been restrained by fiscal policy.)

From 1983 on, there is a much closer correspondence between our targets and actual outcomes, although the actual growth in demand has generally remained somewhat too low to lead to a spurt in growth to recover the ground lost in the 1980–82 recession. Sterling also returned to more reasonable levels, although it did not reattain its estimated FEER until the end of 1986 (and then only temporarily). In 1987 the more balanced macroeconomic policies are at last bearing fruit in the form of a reduction in unemployment, although the tendency of inflation to edge up raises the question as to whether the British economy has yet overcome its habit of translating an excessively large proportion of demand growth into price rises.

Canada

Movements in the Canadian economy tend to reflect those in its large southern neighbor, and the 1980s have been no exception. The Canadian economy held up relatively well in 1980, but the growth in domestic demand was clearly excessive in 1981 when inflation increased and the current account deficit became substantial (figure 9). These developments encouraged the demand squeeze that helped to make the 1982 recession even sharper than the one in the United States (table 8). Since then, the Canadian economy has staged an impressive recovery, combining disinflation with buoyant real growth and, until 1985–86, when a further sharp terms of trade deterioration occurred, a strong balance of payments performance. Unlike the early 1980s, demand growth has been close to our calculated target in recent years although it appears to be somewhat excessive in 1987.

Unlike the US dollar, the Canadian dollar does not seem to have suffered any serious misalignment. It has indeed undergone a significant real effective

---

18. In 1987 British manufacturing production remains below the level of 1979 (and even more below that of 1973), but capacity utilization is reported to be high.

FIGURE 8   **United Kingdom: actual and target rates of growth in domestic demand**

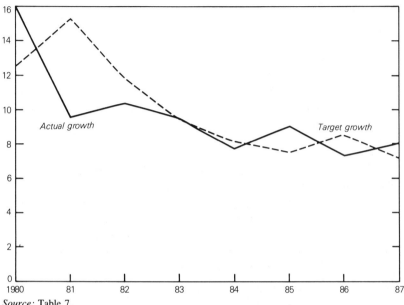

Source: Table 7.

TABLE 7   **United Kingdom: target demand change and actual outcomes, 1980–87** (percentage increase)

Year	Target demand growth $\hat{y}^*$	Actual demand growth $\hat{y}$	Actual increase in nominal income	Increase in GNP g	Increase in GNP deflator $\hat{p}$
1980	12.5	16.0	16.8	−2.5	19.8
1981	15.3	9.5	10.0	−1.3	11.5
1982	11.8	10.4	9.3	1.5	7.7
1983	9.4	9.5	8.6	3.3	5.1
1984	8.1	7.7	7.2	3.1	4.0
1985	7.5	9.0	9.8	3.5	6.1
1986	8.5	7.3	6.5	2.7	3.7
1987	7.4	8.0[a]	8.0[a]	3.3[a]	4.6[a]

Source: Column 1, table A.6; columns 2–5, *OECD Economic Outlook* data base.
a. Estimate from June 1987 *OECD Economic Outlook.*

depreciation during the 1980s, but this was an appropriate response to the major "permanent" deterioration in Canada's terms of trade (Williamson in Wonnacott 1987).

Appraisal

The proposed indicator system would have provided effective warnings against the major mishaps in macroeconomic policy during the first half of the 1980s: the distorted fiscal-monetary mix in the United States and resulting overvaluation of the US dollar, the inadequate growth of domestic demand and resulting overreliance on net exports in Japan, the inadequate growth performance in Germany, the incautious reflation of the Mitterrand administration in France, the delay in disinflating in Italy, the brutal monetary squeeze and resulting sterling overvaluation at the beginning of the Thatcher government, and the excessive seesaw of Canadian demand in 1981-82. The changes the rules would have called for in the international environment would generally have been helpful. Policies in each country would have been pushed toward greater international compatibility, which would have made them more sustainable.

It seems to us rather encouraging that a single formula applied to seven different countries should have produced such apparently sensible results for all of them, even allowing for the fact that we invented the parameters with the objective of generating sensible results. It surely does suggest that a relatively modest measure of agreement on desirable policy strategies could be translated into indicator formulae that would caution against repetition of the sorts of policy errors made in recent years (typically in the wake of a change of government; see Bergsten, 1986a, for an analysis of US postwar history in this regard).

This is not to claim that all of the policy advice implied by the indicators would find ready acceptance even today. We have already pointed to the possibility that some would argue that the severity of the 1982 recession was necessary to defeat inflation. The other implication that seems likely to be controversial is the need for a period of catch-up growth in Europe, particularly in Germany, as implied by the consistent shortfall of actual demand growth behind target demand growth of recent years. This advice makes sense if additional demand would be translated primarily into increased output but not if it would simply stimulate price rises. Since we do not believe that

FIGURE 9   **Canada: actual and target rates of growth in domestic demand**

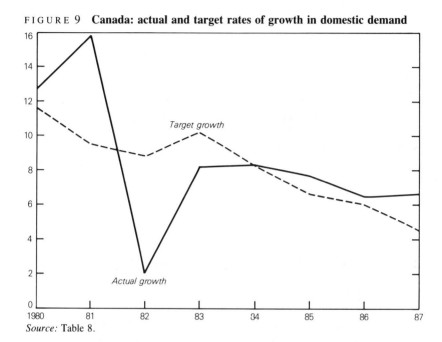

Source: Table 8.

TABLE 8   **Canada: target demand change and actual outcomes, 1980–87**
(percentage increase)

Year	Target demand growth $\hat{y}^*$	Actual demand growth $\hat{y}$	Actual increase in nominal income	Increase in GNP g	Increase in GNP deflator $\hat{p}$
1980	11.6	12.7	12.2	1.5	10.5
1981	9.5	15.8	14.9	3.7	10.8
1982	8.8	2.1	5.3	− 3.3	8.9
1983	10.2	8.2	8.2	3.1	4.9
1984	8.2	8.3	9.3	5.5	3.6
1985	6.6	7.7	7.5	4.0	3.4
1986	6.0	6.5	6.1	3.2	2.8
1987	4.5	6.6[a]	7.0[a]	2.6[a]	4.3[a]

Source: Column 1, table A.7; columns 2–5, *OECD Economic Outlook* data base.
a. Estimate from June 1987 *OECD Economic Outlook*.

Germany is on the brink of rekindling inflation, we believe the advice is sound, but presumably that judgment may not be universally endorsed.

Even if the indicators proposed by our blueprint were adopted, policy could not be expected to fine tune the economy to follow the course mapped out as desirable. Forecasts remain distinctly imperfect, and as long as that is true one must expect that outcomes will deviate from those planned. Nevertheless, an agreed and consistent set of policy objectives could surely be expected to improve the performance of the world economy over what is likely if the oscillations and bickering of the past are perpetuated in the future.

4   Alternative International Monetary Systems

The proposals embodied in the preceding "blueprint" amount to a grand design for international monetary reform. It therefore seems interesting to compare their characteristics with those of alternative possible bases for international monetary organization. The leading contenders, covering both systems that have actually operated in the past and proposals for a reformed system for the future, are classified in figure 10. The classification rests on two distinctions: whether exchange rates are fixed, freely floating, or managed, and whether the system is symmetrical among countries or depends upon a leading (hegemonic) power.

Past Systems

The first organized international monetary system was the gold standard, which was widely adhered to from about 1870 until 1914. In principle, a gold standard is a symmetrical system, with exchange rates being fixed and monetary expansion in all countries being driven by their balance of payments position, while the world money stock is driven by the rate of gold mining. In practice it is now accepted that in many respects the gold standard behaved distinctly asymmetrically, with monetary expansion heavily influenced by

FIGURE 10   **Alternative international monetary systems**

	Fixed exchange rates	Floating exchange rates with national targets	Managed exchanged rates
Symmetry	Gold standard, 1870–1914 Bretton Woods system, 1945–68 McKinnon's proposals	Monetary targets (Friedman's proposals, OECD 1973–85) Nominal income targets	Louvre Blueprint
Hegemony	Dollar standard, 1968–73	—	EMS 1979–

credit expansion and a payments-induced contraction by Britain, the leading economy, precipitating adjustment via terms of trade changes at the expense of the periphery (Triffin 1964).

The interwar years produced a variety of arrangements—floating exchange rates with no agreed rules to govern monetary policy, a brief return to fixed rates with a gold exchange standard, a period when some countries remained on gold while others floated, and finally three years of semistability governed by the Tripartite Agreement of 1936. None of these fit neatly into the classification of figure 10: periods of floating rates were not complemented by any well-defined national targets, the attempt to restore fixed rates was unsuccessful perhaps in part because the system was bigemonic rather than hegemonic or symmetrical, while the Tripartite Agreement belongs in the final column but was again something between hegemonic and symmetrical.

The Bretton Woods system is classified in the top left-hand cell, although in reality it was something of a hybrid. It normally expected the maintenance of fixed exchange rates, but allowed occasional parity changes in the event of "fundamental disequilibrium." Since step changes in exchange rates proved incompatible with high capital mobility, the system is now of only historical interest. It was designed to be symmetrical in the crucial aspects governing the influence on macroeconomic policy, but commenced operating at a time when the world economy was dominated by the United States, and evolved into the hegemonic dollar standard, the decisive break between the two regimes being the abandonment of the gold pool in 1968. The key features of a dollar standard are that the United States selects its monetary policy with a view to domestic stability and other countries peg to the dollar, with the right to change their peg at their unilateral discretion.

Fixed exchange rates were abandoned in favor of floating in 1973, in part because the surplus countries (especially Germany) found US hegemony to be intolerable, and in part because the United States found the nth-currency role assigned it by the dollar standard irksome. Before long most major countries had adopted national money supply targets as the new nominal anchor to replace a fixed exchange rate, thus approximating the policy regime long advocated by Milton Friedman (1953). Such a regime appears to be inherently symmetrical rather than hegemonic. (A single currency may remain the dominant form of international money, as the dollar in fact did, but this does not have major implications for the determination of macroeconomic policy, which is the vital issue at stake in designing an international monetary system.)

By 1979 the European countries had become sufficiently disenchanted with the operation of unmanaged floating to decide to break away and form a "zone of monetary stability," the EMS. Like Bretton Woods, this was designed to be a symmetrical system, with the "divergence indicator" created specifically with that end in view. But in practice it has operated asymmetrically, with the DM rapidly becoming the key currency to which others have to adjust and the system now widely viewed as a mechanism whereby other countries can buy some of the Bundesbank's anti-inflation credibility on the cheap (Giavazzi and Giovannini 1987). The system is described as one of managed rather than fixed exchange rates because realignments have been accepted from the start as a necessary part of the system. Realignments have generally permitted partial compensation for inflation differentials (as well as taking some account of the need for adjustment), so that the EMS has operated as a hybrid of a fixed nominal rate and fixed real rate system. Realignments have generally been sufficiently modest to avoid the speculative pressures that destroyed the Bretton Woods system, although parity changes have occasionally been somewhat wider than the band and have thus risked reviving major speculative crises.

The system of global floating effectively ended with the Plaza Agreement to force the dollar down in September 1985. The float has since then been managed, in the sense that the major countries have cared about their exchange rates and taken actions to influence them. Since the Louvre accord, the G-7 has acted to stabilize exchange rates within agreed "reference ranges," but it has still not agreed on any set of principles of macroeconomic management or formalized agreement in a set of indicators.

Proposed Systems

It seems that there are three main competitors to a system along the lines of our blueprint. One of these, the adoption of fixed exchange rates backed up by a common monetary policy, has long been associated with the name of Ronald McKinnon. The other two both involve a reversion to floating exchange rates. The first of these two proposals involves combining floating exchange rates with fixed monetary growth targets à la Friedman. The other involves combining floating with national nominal income targets; this proposal has received little articulation, but might well command substantial support among American economists.

For some years McKinnon advocated fixed exchange rates and a fixed collective rate of monetary growth by the three major countries, to be achieved by a predetermined rate of domestic credit expansion in each and unsterilized intervention. This would have allowed the distribution of monetary growth to be demand determined and guaranteed the maintenance of fixed exchange rates. Recently McKinnon has modified his proposal to recognize the problems created by variable velocity, and now proposes that the three major countries pursue a collective monetary policy targeted on the preservation of stability in the average price of traded goods (McKinnon forthcoming).

It is interesting to observe that none of the leading proposals envisage reversion to a hegemonic system. It does indeed seem inconceivable that Germany or Japan would be prepared to contemplate accepting the monetary leadership of the United States with no questions asked, as a dollar standard would imply. At the same time, one must recognize that the historical record is not particularly encouraging as to the possibility of operating a genuinely symmetrical system. Ostensibly symmetrical systems—the gold standard, Bretton Woods, the EMS—have in practice relied upon strong leadership by the major power. Building a pluralistic and reasonably symmetrical system will demand a high order of economic statesmanship. Cynics will doubtless conclude that this means the task should not even be attempted.

Another interesting development is the more direct influence over national macroeconomic policies assumed by present-day proposals in comparison with the systems of former days. The gold standard assumed that countries' macroeconomic policies would be influenced indirectly, by the impact of changes in gold reserves. The same vision persisted until the 1970s, when variation in the stock of international reserves was thought of as the critical means by which international action (in the form of SDR allocations) could exert an influence over countries' policies. In contrast, both McKinnon and our blueprint assume that effective policy coordination requires direct international influence over vital national macroeconomic decisions. In this they are in tune with the lead set by the Tokyo summiteers in 1986.

Comparative Characteristics

Figure 11 identifies six key characteristics of an international monetary system, and suggests how all but one of the systems classified in figure 10 perform in terms of each of these criteria. The omitted system involves the reference ranges agreed at the Louvre. The information available on what this may involve is, unfortunately, insufficient as yet to permit informed entries to be made in any of the columns of figure 11. (To be fair, one should add that the Louvre is better regarded as a stage in the construction of a new system rather than as a definitive set of new arrangements.)

The first column of figure 11 deals with whether a system has a built-in mechanism for inflation control. The hegemonic systems at the bottom of the table essentially rely upon responsible behavior by the dominant member economy. All the symmetrical systems above them contain a mechanism for inflation control, although this was weak under the Bretton Woods system, because it depended upon a global reserve shortage to induce countries to pursue less expansionary policies.

A second characteristic of an international monetary system is whether it builds in any mechanism for dampening the world business cycle. Once again, the hegemonic systems rely upon the needs of the hegemonic power being representative of the system as a whole and having the hegemon modify its policies in pursuit of its own interests. Floating rates with national money supply targets are predicated on the assumption that the best defense against the business cycle, at world or national level, is a steady growth of the money supply—a claim that we find unconvincing in view of the recent variability of velocity. The gold standard was supposed to have some modest anticyclical power since gold mining incentives would increase in a recession,

FIGURE 11 **Summary comparison of properties of international monetary systems**

System	Inflation control	Dampens world cycle	Internal balance	Exchange rate changes as adjustment tool	Control of misalignments	Macroeconomic independence
Gold standard	Yes	Modest	No	No	No	No
Bretton Woods	Weak	Yes	Yes	Difficult	Poor	Constrained
McKinnon	Yes	Yes	No	No	No	No
Floating with national money supply targets	Yes	Poor	Poor	Yes	No	Yes
Floating with national nominal income targets	Yes	Yes	Yes	Yes	No	Yes
Blueprint	Yes	Yes	Yes	Yes	Yes	Constrained
Dollar standard	Relies on United States	Relies on United States	Yes for United States, permits for ROW	Permits, except United States	Permits, except United States	Yes for United States; constrained for ROW
European Monetary System	Relies on Germany	Relies on Germany	Yes for Germany; constrained for rest of EMS	Yes	Encourages	Constrained, but less so for Germany

though there is little evidence that this mechanism was effective. Bretton Woods encouraged countries to pursue anticyclical policies. McKinnon's rule would call for faster monetary growth when prices were threatening to fall, in a recession. If the nominal income targets used with floating rates had the same form that we have suggested for use with managed rates, they would have some anticyclical potential as a result of including the deflationary gap among the factors determining the target growth of nominal income. Our blueprint provides also for the average level of world interest rates to be reduced when aggregate (world) nominal income growth falls below target.

The third column in figure 11 shows whether each of the systems permits an individual country to pursue internal balance. Neither the gold standard nor McKinnon's proposals provides for this, although Bretton Woods permitted the use of fiscal policy to this end. Our blueprint would encourage the use of fiscal policy, and permit the use of monetary policy within the constraints implied by the target zone, in the interests of internal balance. Floating with nominal income targets would remove the constraints on the use of monetary policy. Hegemonic systems allow the hegemonic power to adopt policies directed to its own needs. The dollar standard gave a freer hand to the nonhegemonic powers to pursue their own interests than the EMS does.

The fourth criterion is whether the exchange rate can be altered to facilitate the adjustment process when this appears advantageous. This is not possible under a true fixed rate system. Bretton Woods did permit parity changes to that end, although the pressures to deny that parity changes were imminent meant that these were difficult. Floating rates permit such changes, although they do not provide any assurance that rates will actually change in the desired way. The dollar standard also permits such changes, except by the United States, while the EMS encourages them. Our blueprint is even more explicit in expecting such changes.

The fifth criterion is whether the various systems permit control of misalignments. Such control is important not only to achieve macroeconomic objectives but also to preserve an open trading system.

The ability of the exchange rate to change when this can help promote adjustment is a *necessary* condition for this, but it is not *sufficient,* for floating rates can become badly misaligned, as experience has shown. Bretton Woods permitted exchange rate changes in the event of fundamental disequilibrium, although the reluctance to make parity changes meant that serious misalignments arose. McKinnon denies that misalignments could arise under his system because goods arbitrage is supposedly so good, but this is another claim that we find unconvincing. The dollar standard permits the noncenter countries to adjust their exchange rates to eliminate misalignments, although the United States does not have any such freedom. The EMS has encouraged countries to realign rather than allow major misalignments to emerge. Our blueprint places great emphasis on avoiding misalignments and to that end envisages countries choosing target rates with the conscious objective of a correct alignment, preventing the target rates from becoming outdated through differential inflation, changing their targets if fundamental factors create a need for realignment, and changing their interest rates relative to the world average to limit misalignments.

The final column is headed "macroeconomic independence." Typically, such independence may be used for two purposes: to choose an inflation rate independent of the rest of the world, and to pursue a countercyclical policy directed to domestic needs. The latter issue was already discussed under the heading "internal balance." However, a proposal may expect a country to pursue internal balance (as our blueprint indeed does), in which case it presumably does not satisfy those who place great emphasis on countries being free to choose their own policies, even if these are misguided.

Views differ greatly as to the desirability of macroeconomic independence. Indeed, the ability of a country to choose its own inflation rate is viewed by some as a regrettable absence of "external discipline." Thus the great virtue of floating has sometimes been perceived to be the freedom it gives to countries to pursue independent macroeconomic policies, while others have viewed the loss of external discipline over the inflation rate as its great vice.

Whatever one's normative attitude to this question, the facts are that the true fixed rate systems (gold standard and McKinnon) do not permit macroeconomic independence, i.e., do impose strong external discipline, while the floating system permits macroeconomic independence and thus destroys external discipline. Bretton Woods placed some external constraints on its members, the obligation to seek to avoid parity changes and to seek approval for any changes a country did wish to make, but these were less severe than the constraints of a true fixed rate system. The dollar standard permits the United States to select its own macroeconomic policies, to which other countries that wish to peg to the dollar have to conform. The EMS does not give the same degree of independence to Germany, but Germany still has more independence than other members.

Our blueprint is rather different from any of the other systems with regard to this question. The fact that exchange rate targets are defined in real terms, so that the nominal exchange rate target is automatically adjusted in line with differential inflation, means that the traditional form of an external discipline over the inflation rate is absent from the system. However, an agreement to negotiate a target exchange rate, to use monetary policy to limit deviations from that rate, and to pursue a target for the growth of domestic demand (even if the parameters used in calculating that target were a matter of national choice), would involve the acceptance of significant constraints on macroeconomic independence.

In our view, the question of whether macroeconomic independence is formally constrained is of less importance than the question of whether the constraints countries are asked to accept are in their own long-run interest. The macroeconomic independence conferred by floating rates is bought at too high a price if it results in bouts of competitive depreciation (on the model of the 1930s) or appreciation (recall 1973–74, or how other major countries followed the United States in eliminating withholding taxes on nonresident interest income in 1984). Similarly, the external discipline on inflation of a fixed nominal exchange rate is unnecessary, given the alternative discipline of a nominal income (or domestic demand) target.

If one believes that the important issue is whether a regime is in a country's economic interest rather than whether it confers nominal macroeconomic independence, one is led back to examine the entries in the first five columns of figure 11. Since our blueprint is the only system that satisfies all five of those criteria, it seems the natural choice if one believes that all these criteria are important.[19]

5   Some Responses to Critics

The full proposal for policy coordination laid out in this study was first developed in the summer of 1986, circulated in late 1986 in unpublished

---

19. Some of the more subtle differences are not, however, recorded in the table. For example, the only difference there recorded between the blueprint and floating with national nominal income targets concerns the ability of the former but not the latter to control misalignments. But, as noted in the text, the blueprint provides for a stronger anticyclical thrust at the world level (via rule (A) for interest rates) and a constrained, and thus weaker, anticyclical thrust at the national level.

form, and has only recently been published in its more technical form (Edison, Miller, and Williamson 1987). It has not therefore been subject to extensive critical appraisal. Nevertheless, reactions to oral presentations suggest that some of the criticisms directed to the target zone proposal advanced previously by one of the present authors (Williamson 1985) and incorporated in rule (B) of the present proposal continue to trouble some economists. A section of this study is therefore devoted to an explicit confrontation with the critics.

We take up below eight topics on which we are aware of criticism. These topics exclude one frequent refrain, the assertion that the real need is for better policies rather than a reform of the system, for a reason that we trust will be readily apparent to those who have read this far: the dichotomy between a good system and good policies is false (Bergsten 1986b). The purpose of a system is to influence the policies that countries choose to pursue: the relevant question is whether the proposed system will influence policies in a helpful way. (If policies are not to be influenced by the system, then the only possible "system" is the nonsystem under which exchange rates are allowed to float to reconcile the uncoordinated.)

Role of Fiscal Policy

Efforts to reform the exchange-rate system should be preceded by a reform of fiscal policy . . . We need to reform fiscal policy in . . . two senses. First, the [US] budget deficit has to be reduced to a low level so that an occasional deliberate increase in the deficit would not be unthinkable. Second, procedures have to be put in place that would make possible a rapid alteration of fiscal policy, such as a tax cut or increase. Only when fiscal policy can be brought into play to stabilize the economy on a durable growth path should we even consider proposals that would divert monetary policy from its primary domestic goal. (Solomon 1987)

One of the motivations for this study was the desire to synthesize the target zone proposal with the necessary supporting rules for fiscal policy, rather than simply arguing that adoption of target zones would increase the pressure for responsible fiscal policies (as did Williamson 1985, p. 33; 1986, pp. 169–70). We hope that those who share Solomon's eminently sensible views about the crucial importance of an enlightened fiscal policy will feel that if the proposal laid out above were to be adopted it would fully meet their concerns.

It is worth asking whether the needed reforms in fiscal policy are more likely to be accomplished independently (by insisting that a reform of fiscal policy "precede" international monetary reform) or jointly. It happens that the US House of Representatives has earlier in 1987 affirmed that "the actual exchange rate of the dollar cannot be brought into alignment' with its competitive exchange rate unless. . . . the Federal budget deficit is reduced" (section 402[10], HR3, the trade bill). The Competitive Exchange Rate Act incorporated in HR3 goes on to indicate the willingness of the House to support international negotiations for the coordination of economic policy, and implicitly approves the inclusion of US fiscal policy on the agenda of what should be coordinated.

Of course, no one can be sure that the House would not have second thoughts, nor that the Senate would go along, if it came to the crunch and Congress was actually asked to reform the fiscal process as part and parcel of an international monetary reform. But the depth of congressional concern at the US trade deficit suggests that it could at least be expected to look seriously at proposals for fiscal reform that were perceived to be an integral part of measures to remedy the existing deficit and prevent a recurrence. It is not obvious why fiscal reforms introduced independently with a mere hope that the Fed would then treat monetary policy as free to manage the exchange rate, and with no guarantee that those policies would not be nullified by foreign reactions, should have comparable political appeal.

We would also query Solomon's contention that monetary policy should be exclusively devoted to domestic goals during any interim period until fiscal reform has been achieved. When one instrument has to serve two objectives, economists normally argue that the setting of the instrument should be determined by some trade-off between what would be desirable on the basis of each objective independently. A principal purpose of proposing a wide target zone for the exchange rate was to allow monetary policy to continue to be used for domestic stabilization purposes most of the time. Only when this policy threatened truly serious consequences from misalignment would the authorities be expected to give a major weight to the exchange rate.

The Lucas critique (1981) argues that a change in the policy regime can be expected to change the behavior of the private sector. This suggests that sterilized intervention might be made a useful policy instrument able to differentiate the effects of monetary policy on the exchange rate and the domestic economy if the market came to interpret such intervention as a signal of preparedness to make supporting changes in interest rates should the need arise. To preclude this possibility by requiring that monetary policy be exclusively directed to domestic needs appears misguided.

Endorsement of Solomon's basic message regarding the importance of fiscal reform will doubtless raise suspicions in some quarters that we are seeking to reinstate "fine tuning." We do not know whether or not to plead guilty to this charge. If "fine tuning" is interpreted to mean a belief that nominal income can be maintained on a narrowly defined path, we are not so naive. If it is interpreted to mean monthly changes in tax rates or installment credit regulations, then it seems unnecessary and possibly counterproductive as well as utterly improbable. We favor a fiscal policy comprising the maintenance of strong automatic fiscal stabilizers[20] and an annual budgetary process that tries to help sustain the growth of domestic demand on its target path, subject to the medium-run need to avoid an excessive debt buildup and to produce an adequate level of aggregate savings in the economy. To describe this as fine tuning and then be against it because of its label seems rather silly.

Loss of Control of Nominal Variables

Some economists have expressed concern over the target zone proposal on the ground that it implies a loss of control over nominal variables, meaning in particular a loss of control over inflation. For example:

. . . widely accepted principles about the general long-run properties of economies imply that under a real exchange rate rule the authorities no longer control the price level, and that inflation might become unstable (Adams and Gros 1986, p. 472).

What worries Adams and Gros is that monetary policy is being assigned to stabilization of a real variable, the real exchange rate. It is well known that instability results when the chosen value of a real target is a disequilibrium value. The traditional example (Adams and Gros, p. 460) concerns an attempt to target unemployment at a rate lower than the natural rate or NAIRU, which leads to accelerating inflation (Friedman 1968, Phelps 1967). Similarly, an attempt to target a more competitive real exchange rate than the economy

---

20. It might seem redundant to mention this but for the fact that in recent years one member of the G-7, namely Britain, has gone out of its way to suppress the automatic stabilizers with a view to seeking to achieve a target growth path for the public sector borrowing requirement.

can sustain could lead to accelerating inflation as the payments surplus is monetized, but the authorities depreciate the exchange rate whenever prices rise and thus thwart adjustment of the surplus.

This problem has been familiar to supporters of real exchange rate rules for some years (Williamson 1981, pp. 392–94). The most obvious moral is the importance of ensuring that the real target is one that is consistent with macroeconomic equilibrium. One can interpret the breakdown of the Keynesian demand management that enjoyed such spectacular success in the 1950s and first half of the 1960s as a consequence of the failure of the authorities to admit that circumstances had changed in a way that dictated modification of their real targets (specifically, that the NAIRU had risen). The monetarist defense against this danger is to abandon real targets altogether and set the economy on automatic pilot by targeting only monetary variables. But, since the targets that actually matter are real targets, this is to throw out the baby with the bathwater unless one has great confidence that the economy will promptly achieve equilibrium values for variables like unemployment and the real exchange rate once it has been set on automatic pilot. The experience of countries like Argentina, Britain, and Chile that tried to install a monetarist automatic pilot at the turn of the decade does not instill great confidence in the likely speed of convergence to equilibrium.

The alternative defense against the danger of setting a disequilibrium real target is to build some feedback mechanism into policy design that will modify the real targets if they start to generate unstable behavior. The most obvious way of doing this in the context of a real exchange rate rule is to monitor the appropriateness of the target real exchange rate in the light of the development of inflation and the current account. It is not necessarily optimal to appreciate the target real exchange rate in response to any acceleration in core inflation; the appropriate response might be a rise in the target unemployment rate, or even an incomes policy. But some response is necessary. Which one should be chosen, or what combination of them, depends upon whether the current account balance is larger or smaller than desired and how badly the labor market is working.

While such discretionary changes in targets should certainly be made promptly as and when the evidence indicates them to be needed, our proposed policy rules contain a fallback mechanism to preclude any possibility that inflation accelerates indefinitely even if the authorities were again to be as slow to adjust to unfavorable changes in the environment as they were in 1965–75. This is the nominal income rule, and in particular the provision that inflation be only partially accommodated. This ensures that an acceleration of inflation would lead to a tightening of fiscal policy (Miller and Williamson 1987; see also appendix B). The basic point is that a fiscal tightening changes the real conditions that are assumed to be constant in the Adams-Gros analysis and this permits inflation to be stabilized even without a change in the real exchange rate target.

A variant on the complaint that the proposed regime lacks a nominal anchor (which it does not) is that it assigns a monetary variable (the interest rate) to control a real variable (the real exchange rate) and a real variable (fiscal policy) to control a nominal variable (nominal income). This charge is valid at the national level, although at the world level interest rates are assigned the role of stabilizing nominal income. But the question that needs raising is whether there is any theoretical reason for believing that real and nominal variables *should* be assigned to real and nominal targets, respectively. Is this not another "invalid dichotomy" (Patinkin 1965)? Mundell (1971) once *assumed* that monetary policy could be tightened to bring inflation under control while fiscal policy was loosened to sustain real output, but not a shred of evidence was presented to justify the basic assumption that in a closed economy the two policies would have different effects on prices and output, rather than being alternative methods of influencing nominal demand. In fact the major difference between them comes only in an open economy and arises from their differing impact on the exchange rate, the very difference that is exploited by our proposed assignment.

A more concrete complaint against the target zone proposal is that it would have precluded the successful disinflation of the early 1980s:

There is a proclivity of the habitués of international financial markets to see exchange-rate-oriented monetary policy as the panacea for exchange rate problems. This is particularly clear in the growing cry for exchange rate target zones, whether rigid or of the Williamson kind, that is, with soft bumpers and bleepers. The problem with this recommendation is twofold. First, it is quite clear that with exchange-rate-oriented monetary policy the U.S. would not have been able to have the disinflation that in fact took place. Certainly for stabilization periods it is an inappropriate recommendation. But worse yet, for the U.S. the exchange-rate-oriented monetary policy would have meant the reckless monetization of gigantic budget deficits. (Dornbusch 1986, pp. 12–13.)

This charge is unconvincing, even if it did not come from an economist who is urging a further 30 percent fall in the dollar (Dornbusch 1987) from a level already almost 20 percent below where it was in 1983, with inflation running at a similar rate.[21] Note first that rule (A) provides for an anti-inflationary use of monetary policy at the global level. Thus a common commitment to fight inflation, as opposed to the export of inflation that helped the United States to get inflation down quickly at the cost of a horrendous trade deficit, would have been encouraged. Note second that the wide band would provide scope for a country that wished to pursue a more vigorous disinflationary policy than its partners to tighten up its monetary policy more. Third, if that was not enough differential tightening, it would have the option of tightening up fiscal policy too.

The one thing that would have involved a flagrant breach of the rules is the policy the United States actually pursued, of combating inflation by a very tight monetary policy while sabotaging the effort by a lax fiscal policy that induced a very high exchange rate, a policy directly responsible for the main danger currently overhanging the world economy (the danger of a "hard landing" by the US economy). In the nature of things, no one can be sure that a confident new administration—like the Reagan administration in its first two or three years—would have abided by international obligations proscribing the policy mix that it in fact chose. But it is unreasonable to assert as an incontrovertible fact that an agreed set of international rules would have had no effect.

The United States does not always abide by its obligations under the General Agreement on Tariffs and Trade (GATT), but the existence of these rules makes it easier for the President to resist protectionist pressures. In the same way, one can reasonably expect that at the very least the existence of an agreed set of macroeconomic policy obligations would have tilted the political debate into taking increased account of the need for international compatibility (and thus long-run sustainability). And it is simply not true that President Reagan's views on tax increases ruled out all possibilities of change: he has in fact signed bills involving significant tax rises twice since taking office, in 1982 and 1984.

Imported Inflation

A particular concern of many Germans appears to be that a target zone system would make it impossible to maintain price stability in Germany if

---

21. Dornbusch's complaint about the danger of aborting disinflation referred specifically to 1983.

other countries, notably the United States, started once again to inflate at a worrying rate. For example, in a speech (in German) in Munich on 4 February 1986, Helmut Schlesinger, Deputy Governor of the Bundesbank, argued that central banks would not use the full width of a target zone and that as a result ''one would practically have fixed exchange rates with all the problems this means for a country and its economy: in the final phase, an inflation machine.''

The foundation for this concern is German experience in the later years of the Bretton Woods system. In those years Germany found that its more successful anti-inflation policy led to growing competitiveness, given its fixed exchange rate, and thus increasing current account surpluses. The resulting inflow of foreign exchange was much magnified whenever market expectations of an imminent revaluation of the DM, to limit the increasing competitiveness, were aroused. Sterilization of the inflow was difficult in the short run and ultimately impracticable, implying that it was impossible to prevent inflation from developing. Thus, Germany felt that its attempt to prop up the Bretton Woods system led directly to its bout of inflation in the early 1970s.

Although a greater willingness to revalue promptly might have eased its situation, we have little quarrel with this diagnosis. Nevertheless, we do not believe that it provides a reason for opposing a target zone system. On the contrary, our proposals have been designed in order inter alia to ensure that no country is forced to import inflation as Germany did in the early 1970s. The key differences between the Bretton Woods system and the target zone proposal which would preclude the latter from serving as an engine for importing inflation comparable to the former are:

• The nominal exchange rate target would automatically be appreciated as inflation took hold in other countries, thus preventing an unwanted growth in competitiveness as a by-product of differential inflation.

• The exchange rate could appreciate within the wide zone in response to a tightening of monetary policy if inflationary pressures developed in other countries, thus relieving the buildup in foreign demand and also bringing an anti-inflationary fall in the cost of imports.

• Under the comprehensive proposals for policy coordination presented in this study, other countries would be subject to guidelines on their policies designed to preclude their developing strong inflationary pressures in the short run or a strong inflationary momentum in the long run.

If the German concern that they might be forced to import inflation were valid, it would be a very strong objection indeed. But in fact these three fundamental differences to the Bretton Woods system mean that the danger that a country will be forced to import inflation is virtually zero. On the contrary, US willingness to embrace such a set of rules would provide the strongest assurance that stability-minded countries can possibly hope for against an American attempt to inflate away its accumulating debt.

Volatility Transferred?

It is sometimes argued that any measure that reduces the volatility of exchange rates is likely to increase the volatility of some other variable. The usual candidate is the interest rate, although Frenkel (1987, pp. 207–8) also mentions the labor market. The question is then asked as to why there is any presumption that such a transfer of volatility would be desirable.

The implicit model underlying the question seems to be that there is an unchanging amount of uncertainty that has to be absorbed through the volatility of one or other variable, giving rise to a direct trade-off between volatility of the exchange rate and volatility of the interest rate (or some other variable). If this is correct, the normal presumption would be that some mixture of interest rate and exchange rate volatility would be the least harmful way of absorbing the volatility inherent in the system. The target zone system allows for that, though with an unconventional presumption that exchange rates should bear relatively more of the variability when shocks are small and relatively less when shocks are large (that is implied by the wide zone).

In fact, however, the underlying proposition is highly dubious. Anything that ensures that governmental policies are consistent and better understood by the public—whether this refers to different policies of the same government, to the intertemporal consistency of a single government's policies, or to the policies of different governments—can be expected to reduce the total amount of uncertainty in the system and thus would potentially be able to reduce the volatility of *both* variables. The policy regime proposed in this study is, of course, intended both to ensure policy consistency and to improve public understanding of policy.

In the light of experience of recent years, few economists are now willing to assert dogmatically that foreign exchange markets are efficient and free of speculative runs. It has been shown that the statistical tests that used to be interpreted as demonstrating the efficiency of the foreign exchange market are almost unable to discriminate against the competing hypothesis of periodic "fads" (Poterba and Summers 1987). Indeed, the inability of any respectable theory to explain the final run-up of the dollar from mid-1984 to February 1985, coupled with the hearsay evidence that many investors putting money into the dollar in those months were impressed by journalistic tales of the "superdollar" that defied the laws of economics, make a strong case for arguing the importance of speculative bubbles in the foreign exchange market. It is entirely possible that speculative bubbles, unlike informed arbitrage, can be stopped by official action without paying a price by moving the interest rate.

None of this is intended to deny that exchange rate management will on occasion require a willingness to change interest rates. Rule (B) means what it says. But the Dutch experience in maintaining a currency in a rather tight exchange rate band (the 2¼ percent margins of the EMS) for eight years without exchange controls gives a foretaste of what might be expected. The Dutch have on occasion had to raise interest rates sharply to maintain the guilder within the EMS against market expectations of a possible devaluation. But such changes have quickly restored confidence, so that the periods of high interest rates have been brief. Overall, Dutch interest rates have been neither particularly high nor volatile. The looser structure of a target zone system gives even less reason to expect that interest rates would be particularly volatile within such a system. Occasional increases may be needed to restore confidence when exchange rates threaten to breach target zones, but, provided that the target rates being defended are not disequilibrium rates and that other policies are consistent, there is little reason to fear that high rates would need to last long.

Estimating the Target Exchange Rate

Some critics have pointed to the difficulties in estimating the equilibrium exchange rates that might serve as appropriate targets, and the necessary additional step of achieving international agreement on those estimates, as a reason for avoiding commitment to a target zone system. Some, such as Frenkel and Goldstein (1986), have even suggested that the appropriate concept of the equilibrium exchange rate is open to question.

On the latter issue, Frenkel and Goldstein mention three candidates. The first is purchasing power parity (PPP). This they rightly dismiss on the grounds that the real exchange rate should adjust in response to real shocks, that PPP has been a dismal empirical failure, and that the results of PPP comparisons are sensitive to choice among alternative price indices and base periods.

The second candidate is to estimate a structural model of exchange rate determination that relates the nominal exchange rate to fundamentals and then insert desired paths for the explanatory fundamental variables into the equation. The overwhelming problem with this approach is the empirical failure of structural models of exchange rate determination (Meese and Rogoff 1983).

The third method is what they term the ''underlying balance approach,'' previously used by one of the present authors to calculate fundamental equilibrium exchange rates (Williamson 1985). The attempt here is to identify the real exchange rates that would equate the cyclically adjusted current account balance to normal capital flows in the medium term.

In our judgment the shortcomings of the first two approaches are so substantial that the quest for target zones is likely to be fruitless if the third approach cannot be made operational.[22] This indicates the importance of a critical scrutiny of the Frenkel-Goldstein evaluation of the underlying balance method.

They acknowledge three advantages of this approach for application in a system of target zones. First, it recognizes that judgments about the appropriateness of exchange rates depend on anticipated future macroeconomic policies as well as lagged effects of past exchange rates. Second, it acknowledges that a sustainable payments position need not imply a zero current account balance. Third, it ensures (at least in principle) that the computed exchange rate targets are consistent across countries.

Frenkel and Goldstein go on to make four criticisms of the underlying balance approach, some of which we regard as much more serious than others. One ''problem'' that does not trouble us concerns their charge that ''the underlying balance approach . . . is not well suited to the analysis and diagnosis of the *mix* of macroeconomic policies. . . . [because the approach] cannot distinguish among policy mixes that yield the same output and inflation

---

22. It was the hope of demonstrating the possibility of making this approach operational that led Williamson (1985) to calculate a set of FEERs for the major currencies.

paths.'' It is true that a balance of payments target does not by itself pin down the need for a specific mix of monetary and fiscal policies. In our paradigm, the output and inflation paths are pinned down by the requirement for internal balance, and the *combination* of objectives determines both the overall stance and the mix of monetary and fiscal policy. The need for the extra input of internal balance has been quite explicitly laid out in Williamson's previous work (1985, pp. 27–28, and in Wonnacott 1987, pp. 165–66).

Another complaint is that the large trade models used to implement the underlying balance approach pay little attention to financial variables or to the distinction between expected and unexpected values of variables, making the approach remote from the mechanisms that determine market exchange rates. This criticism also seems misconceived. FEERs are normative constructs, not forecasts. They are then used to guide financial policies, as laid out above. Market mechanisms are relevant in determining what policies are needed to achieve FEERs, not in estimating them.

A third difficulty relates to the operational complexity of the underlying balance approach. We accept the truth of this complaint, but would retort that the IMF (as well as one of the present authors) has long undertaken such calculations from time to time. This suggests that the task is not unmanageable.

However, the problem on which they place primary emphasis is altogether more serious. This is the difficulty in estimating, or indeed in defining, the concept of ''normal'' net capital flows to which the current account should adjust. Yet, as they say:

Estimates of these capital flows play a key role in the estimate of the equilibrium real exchange rate. The reasons why the concept is so slippery include the following: (i) While private saving rates are reasonably stable over time and across countries, the geographic loci of *perceived* investment opportunities are not; the latter depend on a wide set of expected policies in both the origin and host countries—many of which can change precipitately. (ii) Various controls on capital flows make it difficult to determine what is ''normal,'' especially when these controls change over time. (iii) Acquisition of foreign assets subjects the holder to risks (for example, expropriation risk) that are fundamentally different from those associated with domestic assets, and therefore consideration of such risks may limit exposure even when average real rates of return on foreign assets are high. (iv) Large changes in government fiscal positions, and drastic shifts in private portfolio composition, can lead to large swings in observed capital flows, the duration of which is highly uncertain. The end result of all this is that estimates of ''normal'' net capital flows for the likely participants in a target zone system are subject to a considerable margin of error. (Frenkel and Goldstein 1986, p. 657–58)

This is indeed an underresearched subject, on which we plan to do more work in future. Even with the present state of knowledge, however, it is possible to make rough-and-ready estimates and sustain a semitechnical debate. In the first place, one clearly wants the targeted capital flow to be sustainable rather than threatening a progressive increase in the ratio of external debt to other relevant magnitudes (like GNP or exports). This places a fairly definite limit on the size of acceptable current account deficits in the medium term. Second, we can readily identify macroeconomic circumstances that tend to make it rational for a country to import capital: unusually high rates of return on investment, due, for example, to resource discoveries or an increasing level of skill in the labor force, a low capital-labor ratio, or a growing population.

Admittedly, there is no formula that permits translation of such criteria into an objective number for the normal flow of capital, but those who believe it is better to be roughly right than precisely wrong may nonetheless be prepared to make their own guesstimates, as Williamson has done in estimating FEERs (1985, pp. 22–26, and in Wonnacott 1987, pp. 163–65). It might be difficult to reach agreement if these figures were needed to determine a narrow exchange rate zone, but, given that market rates are in any event to be allowed to diverge substantially from the target, one has to be rather pessimistic about the willingness to strike political compromises in order to accept these difficulties as decisive obstacles to calculating exchange rate targets.

It is of course perfectly true that pinpoint estimates of FEERs are not to be taken seriously. That is another reason for advocating wide target zones: there is no point in using monetary policy to defend a target that might be wrong.

Speculation

If in the 1980s a system of target zones for exchange rates had been in opera-tion. . . Exchange rates would have hit the limits of the zone, speculators would have had a field day, and the system would have broken down (Haberler 1986, p. 4).

The recurring speculative crises of the adjustable peg under Bretton Woods resulted from the system's proclivity to offer one-way bets. Each government accepted the obligation to defend a narrow band around a fixed nominal exchange rate (parity) until further notice, but reserved the right to change the parity. Those fixed rates periodically became disequilibrium rates (even if they were not to begin with), either through real shocks or more typically through differential inflation. Since governments were supposed to maintain fixed parities except *in extremis,* they could hardly propose a parity change before it was obvious to all that a change was necessary. But when the market came to realize that a change was needed, a switch out (in) offered the prospect of substantial overnight gains if the currency was devalued (revalued) and the central bank was obliged to buy (sell) back its foreign exchange reserves at a higher price than it had sold (bought) them, at negligible risk (because of the narrow band) if the parity was unchanged. This was the famous one-way bet. To offer speculators a one-way bet is indeed to give them a field day.

The proposals developed in this study, including target zones, have been designed to minimize the danger of offering one-way bets. This is hardly surprising inasmuch as one of the present authors was an early exponent of the view that capital mobility would make the adjustable peg unviable (Williamson 1965, p. 8) and subsequently a harsh critic of the Committee of Twenty's effort to wish away the speculative obstacles to restoration of the adjustable peg (Williamson 1977, ch.5).

The key difference stems from virtual elimination of the danger that the authorities will be called on to defend a disequilibrium rate, as a result of the following features:

● The provision for automatic adjustment of nominal exchange rate targets in the light of inflation (which results from the specification of FEERs as *real* exchange rates), thus guaranteeing that the targets will not be made obsolete by differential inflation.

● The call for regular review of the appropriateness of the real exchange rate targets in the light of new developments in the world economy and new information on balance of payments developments.

● The width of the zone, which provides ample scope to ensure that the equilibrium exchange rate falls within the zone even given the serious problems that arise in estimating FEERs correctly.

● The possible provision of soft buffers, which means that *in extremis,* if a major shock changed an equilibrium rate by enough to push it outside the zone, the authorities would be entitled to cease defending the zone temporarily while they appraised whether it was appropriate to change the zone or to change their policies to push the rate back within the zone.

The wide zone is relevant in two other ways, besides reducing the probability that the authorities will be called on to defend a disequilibrium rate. One is that it greatly increases the potential cost of speculation on a parity change that does not occur. (With the old 2 percent band of Bretton Woods, the most that a speculator could possibly lose was the 2 percent that would be involved in a rebound of the rate to the other side of the band. By the same token, the potential cost under 20 percent target zones would be 10 times as large, implying that no bet would be one-way.) The other is that it would permit needed changes in target rates to occur without forcing discontinuous changes in market rates. As was established long ago in the literature on the crawling peg (Johnson in Halm 1970, ch. 32), the condition for a change in parity to take place without offering abnormal gains is that the size of the parity change be less than the width of the band (since then the central bank cannot be required to buy its foreign exchange back at a higher price than it had sold it). It seems incredible to suppose that jumps in target rates of more than 20 percent would ever be called for, and certainly not if target rates were reviewed regularly.

Yet a further crucial difference between Bretton Woods and the target zone proposal lies in the different instruments that would be used to defend the zones. Under Bretton Woods the principal instrument used was sterilized intervention, which left the incentive to shift funds unchanged and automatically replaced speculative ammunition as it was used. The target zone proposal envisages the use of interest rates (which is much the same as unsterilized intervention), thus altering the incentives in a stabilizing way and not replacing spent ammunition.

The importance of these factors is illustrated by the success of the European Monetary System. Most advocates of floating exchange rates were highly skeptical of the viability of the EMS when it was founded in 1979. In the event, it has not been totally free of speculative pressures because the markets have at times anticipated (sometimes, though not always, correctly) that central rates were likely to be changed by more than the width of the band. Nevertheless, the somewhat wider bands, the smaller size of changes in central rates, and the greater willingness to allow interest rates to be changed to defend exchange rates have made speculative pressures far less damaging than they became in the later years of Bretton Woods. To assert that a system incorporating even wider zones and more regular small parity changes would revert to the speculative problems of Bretton Woods is unconvincing, to say the least.

The Width of the Zone

While most criticisms of target zones have come from economists who prefer to continue to allow exchange rates to float, one particular aspect of the target zone proposal worries those who prefer fixed or pegged rates. This is the suggestion that zones might be as wide as ± 10 percent.

Several points have been advanced in the course of the preceding argument in favor of wide zones:

● The need to allow substantial latitude for monetary policy to be used for managing domestic nominal income, in view of the political inflexibility of fiscal policy in some countries and its possible perverse short-run impact on nominal income in others.

● The difficulty in calculating reliable estimates of exchange rate targets, particularly in view of the ambiguity surrounding the concept of the ''normal'' capital flow.

● The undesirability of having central banks sacrifice their credibility, or their taxpayers' money, by defending disequilibrium targets.

● The need to provide an adequate margin to permit parity changes to be made without forcing changes in market exchange rates.

The counterargument against such wide zones is that they undermine the benefits that agreed exchange rate targets are supposed to bring. They may do little to focus expectations, and for that reason may not reduce total uncertainty much, with the result that interest rates remain high and exchange rates remain volatile as well. International differences may remain about where exchange rates should be within the zone. Movements within the band might still generate noticeable misalignments.

It is wrong, however, to suggest that target zones of ± 20 percent would have had a negligible effect in limiting the size of misalignments. Even if most governments did not like the idea of being near the middle of the zone most of the time, our estimates imply that all of the independently floating currencies have been substantially more than 10 percent away from their FEER at some point in the past decade. Both the dollar and the pound have exceeded their estimated FEERs by something on the order of 40 percent. Even currencies whose effective exchange rates have been stabilized by membership in the EMS have become misaligned by around 10 percent.

Nevertheless, it may well prove sensible to contemplate target zones narrower than ± 10 percent in the future, once the world has had a period of sufficient stability to get a better feel for the exchange rate levels that will produce satisfactory payments outcomes in the medium term. That would much reduce the second and third reasons given above for desiring wide zones. The fourth reason is certainly satisfied by ± 5 percent. Thus the real issue will be whether a zone of ± 5 percent or so would give adequate freedom for monetary policy to control nominal demand, an issue that will surely depend upon the extent to which fiscal policy can be made more flexible and effective.[23]

Shooting the Messenger

There are those who view exchange rates as an important gauge which provides valuable information about current as well as prospective policies. According to this view, manipulating the exchange rate by intervention and blaming the volatility, unpredictability, and misalignment on the monetary system makes as much sense as blaming the messenger for conveying bad news. (Frenkel 1987)

Analogies are sometimes amusing but often misleading. This one certainly is, for two reasons, of which the first is that exchange rates are a bad messenger.

An appreciation may be due to a real shock that needs a real appreciation, a successful counterinflation policy that merits a nominal appreciation, a rise in interest rates provoked by higher inflation, a rise in interest rates provoked by something else, a speculative bubble, or sundry other causes. Indeed, the point has been made with great eloquence by Frenkel (1987):

---

23. EMS experience in managing with narrow bands is not very relevant in this context, inasmuch as Europe tends to experience a common business cycle and the need for divergent contracyclical monetary policies is therefore less within Europe than between the three major blocs.

Over the past few years we were told that "The dollar *fell* because the money supply grew faster than expected—thereby generating inflationary expectations," but on another occasion we were told that "The dollar *rose* because the money supply grew faster than expected—thereby generating expectations that the Fed is likely to tighten up and raise interest rates." On another date we were told that "The dollar *fell* since the budget deficit exceeded previous forecasts—thereby generating inflationary expectations on the belief that the Fed will have to monetize the deficit," but, on another occasion we were told that "The dollar *rose* since the budget deficit exceeded previous forecasts—thereby generating expectations that government borrowing needs will drive up interest rates since the Fed is unlikely to give up its firm stance." On yet another day we were told that "The dollar *fell* since oil prices fell—thereby hurting Mexico and other debt-ridden oil-producing countries whose bad fortune may bring about the collapse of important US banks," but, on another occasion we were told that "The dollar *rose* since oil prices fell—thereby helping the debt-ridden oil-consuming countries whose improved fortune will help the vulnerable position of important US banks." More recently the dollar changed again, and this time the explanation was a bit more sophisticated: "The dollar changed because the extent of the revision of the estimated GNP growth rate was smaller than the expected revision of previous forecasts of these estimates." One cannot but sympathize with the difficulties shared by newspaper reporters and financial analysts who feel obligated to come up with daily explanations for daily fluctuations of exchange rates, and one can only imagine the deep frustration that yielded the recent headline in the *International Herald Tribune* according to which "The dollar rose on no news."

It is something of a mystery as to how the same Frenkel who wrote the above passage can believe that the exchange rate is such a reliable messenger that it must not be tampered with.

The second reason the analogy of the exchange rate as a messenger is misleading is that messengers influence actions only indirectly, by altering the information available to decisionmakers. Exchange rates, in contrast, are a critical determinant of the incentive to produce for the domestic rather than for the external market and to buy from domestic rather than foreign suppliers. Indeed, the (real) exchange rate has often been described as the most important relative price in any economy (and nowadays that may even be true of the United States).

A misaligned exchange rate is not a harmless messenger but a dangerous saboteur of economic performance. Saboteurs have traditionally been shot. Misaligned exchange rates should be dealt with equally forcefully.

6 Concluding Remarks

In this study we have sought to lay out a set of proposals that would put flesh on the indicators exercise initiated by the G-7 heads of state at Tokyo in 1986. Our blueprint incorporates the target zone proposal, but, in accordance with the apparent willingness of the summit leaders to envisage more ambitious measures of policy coordination, goes beyond exchange rates to detail how comprehensive macroeconomic policy coordination could be organized.

The communiqué following the Tokyo summit listed 10 variables as suitable indicators: the growth rate of GNP, inflation, interest rates, unemployment, the fiscal deficit, current account and trade balances, monetary growth rates, international reserves, and exchange rates. Of these 10, our blueprint treats 4 as targets (growth, inflation, unemployment, and the current account), 2 as instruments (interest rates and the fiscal deficit), 1 as an intermediate target (exchange rates), and drops 3 as redundant (monetary growth, the trade balance, and international reserves).[24] We add 1 extra intermediate target, the rate of growth of domestic demand in nominal terms.

The intermediate targets are chosen with a view to securing a sustainable and satisfactory macroeconomic balance in the medium term. Thus the growth in domestic demand would be calculated to bring the economy gradually toward the highest sustainable level of employment and an acceptably low inflation rate (as well as to support the balance of payments adjustment process). The targets for real effective exchange rates would be chosen with the intention of securing an agreed and sustainable set of current account balances in the medium run. These targets would need to be consistent not only internationally, but also with the structural fiscal stance of each country.

The $2n$ intermediate targets would be pursued by the following three assignment rules:

- *The average level* of world (real) short-term interest rates should be revised up (down) if aggregate growth of nominal income threatens to exceed (fall short of) the sum of the target growth of nominal demand for the participating countries.

---

24. It has been rumored that the 10 indicators were reduced to 7 at Venice, but no announcement has been made as to which were deleted.

• *Differences* in short-term interest rates among countries should be revised when necessary to reinforce exchange market intervention to prevent the deviation of currencies from their target ranges.

• National *fiscal policies* should be revised with a view to achieving national target rates of growth of domestic demand.

We have spoken of a set of "rules" for policy coordination. Initially, at least, these are unlikely to be more than "guidelines" that create presumptions of desirable policy measures, if for no other reason than the continuing reluctance of the major countries to sacrifice nominal sovereignty. (The world is too interdependent for countries to have much real economic sovereignty in any event.) But there is a good economic reason as well as this debatable political reason as to why the obligations of a system of coordination should take the form of presumptive guidelines rather than rigid rules. This economic reason is that, however hard one tries to design rules that will remain appropriate under a wide range of circumstances, it is inconceivable that one will succeed in covering every contingency that may arise. A system needs the flexibility to allow its members to respond to exceptional circumstances without jeopardizing its continued existence.

Nevertheless, guidelines will not realize their full potential unless they are sufficiently firm to ensure that countries do indeed follow them unless exceptional circumstances dictate otherwise. This is not just, and perhaps not even primarily, because the interests of other countries will be threatened if each participant is free to follow the guidelines only when this is convenient to its perceived short-run national interest. It is also because it is to the benefit of each individual country if its government is able to make a commitment which its own public will find credible.[25] (For example, it is less costly to reduce inflation if the public believes a government commitment to reduce it.) A set of internationally monitored rules can provide a mechanism through which governments can make such precommitments, provided that the public believes they will be abandoned only when the other participating governments are convinced that exceptional circumstances have arisen and

---

25. There is now an extensive economic literature on "time consistency" and the advantage a government gains by being able to provide binding undertakings regarding future policy. See Fischer (1986) for a recent survey.

that the proposed policy modification does not contravene the spirit of the original commitment.

Of course, one can hardly expect a set of governments, let alone all the other actors in the political process of economic policymaking, to make a definitive commitment to a set of untested rules, or even guidelines. In the first instance one should probably hope for no more than that the common endorsement of a set of guidelines should tilt the political debate toward greater recognition of the international implications of national policies (Bergsten 1986b). But even this might be helpful in limiting the sort of macroeconomic misfortunes that the world has witnessed repeatedly since the breakdown of Bretton Woods, for in many, perhaps most, cases the first manifestation of unsustainable macroeconomic policies is on the external front. (Recall the appreciation of the dollar or pound sterling in the face of unsustainable fiscal and monetary policies respectively, the French external deficit that ballooned following the initial Mitterrand reflation, or the excessive Japanese and German surpluses that signaled weakness in domestic demand.) As and when the guidelines prove their worth, one may hope that they will become established as a feature of the political landscape that limits political debate to policies that make macroeconomic sense.

Exchange rate targeting, as envisaged in the target zone proposal, is a first step. It can reasonably be expected to avoid exchange rate misalignments caused by speculative bubbles,[26] and that is a worthwhile gain given the extent to which sheer irrationality in the foreign exchange market seems to have occurred, but it could not in itself prevent misalignments caused by divergent fiscal policies. Williamson (1986, pp. 169–70) argued explicitly that a commitment to exchange rate targets embodied in international agreements might help the political process to achieve necessary adjustments in fiscal policies.

Obviously, however, it would be far better if the principles on which those fiscal adjustments should be made were themselves to be the subject of an international understanding. It is even more clear that objectives of policy coordination other than the avoidance of misalignments could not be advanced without an extension of agreement beyond the pattern of exchange rates.

---

26. The main reason for believing this to be important is that no one has provided an explanation for the final months of the dollar's runup, from mid-1984 until February 1985, when the interest differential in favor of the US dollar was declining, except that it was a speculative bubble generated by extrapolative expectations formed by the dollar's earlier rise.

Exchange rate targeting does nothing to increase the assurance that the level of world short-term interest rates is set in accordance with the needs of the world economy. It does not ensure that countries will pursue responsible and mutually consistent demand-management policies. It does not even do much to secure a better set of current account outcomes (recall the first simulation in appendix C).

Indeed, there are potential dangers in targeting exchange rates in isolation. The one emphasized in the economic literature was the danger that the Federal Reserve might be forced to monetize the budget deficit by a commitment to keep the dollar down within a target zone (Dornbusch 1986, Frenkel 1987, Solomon 1987). The analagous German concern is that a commitment to keep the dollar up within a target zone might require large-scale intervention or monetary expansion and thus revive the specter of imported inflation. The Williamson version of the target zone proposal contained an escape valve (the soft buffers) to protect against the first threat and a series of provisions (wide margins, automatic nominal appreciation for low-inflation countries, and the right to fiscal restraint) designed to deflect the second. But not all forms of exchange rate targeting are immune to these dangers.

In particular, one needs to ask whether the Louvre accord might fall prey to such dangers. Unfortunately, this seems by no means impossible. The narrow bands and nominal specification of the exchange rate target deprive Germany of two major defenses against imported inflation, though the soft buffers evidently embodied in the Louvre accord do provide an alternative form of protection. Worse still, the three major countries are committed to reference ranges that nobody believes to be consistent with a reduction of their current account imbalances to sustainable levels on the basis of existing policies. Without a further cut in the US fiscal deficit, and corresponding action to increase demand in the rest of the world, it still seems all too likely that at some stage confidence will collapse and the US dollar will experience a further sharp decline (Marris 1987).

On the other hand, there is reason to believe that the G-7 authorities now understand the dangers of defending disequilibrium exchange rates. The soft buffers of the Louvre reference ranges, the apparent pro tem. quality of the agreed targets, and the failure to publish the ranges, will all make it relatively easy to beat a graceful retreat when the time comes. The danger of this is, however, that the authorities may erode their credibility before the time when they need to stand up to strong market pressure in order to prevent the major overshoot of the dollar on the down side that seems all too likely at some stage. A stronger, and public, commitment to limit exchange rates within much wider zones would thus have been preferable. (One can understand that political practicalities—notably the sensitivity of the Japanese to accepting an exchange rate below $1 = ¥ 150—may have ruled out a realistic lower bound for the dollar for the time being, but this may well prove a very short-sighted concern.)

In short, the Louvre accord does not assure the world economy a soft landing from the dangers created by the peculiar mix of economic policies adopted in the years 1981–85. It did something to move the system in a hopeful direction, but much of the blueprint remains to be put in place.

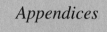

Appendices

Appendix A   Targets for the Growth in Demand

The discussion in section 2 suggested that each country should pursue a target rate of growth for the nominal value of domestic demand that may be expressed as

$$\hat{y}^* = \bar{g} + \hat{p}^* + \alpha(d_{t-1} - d^*) + \beta(\hat{p}_{t-1} - \hat{p}^*) + \gamma(b_{t-1} - b^*)/y,$$

where y = domestic demand (nominal)
$\bar{g}$ = estimated growth rate of productive potential
d = deflationary gap, the excess of potential output over actual output
p = price level
b = current account balance
$\hat{}$ = rate of change
$*$ = a target value.

The first two terms provide for a steady-state growth of domestic demand equal to the rate of growth of productive potential plus the acceptable rate of inflation. The third term adds a fraction α of any excess of the deflationary gap over the level d^* needed to secure the desired reduction in inflation.

In the illustrative calculation of what targets for demand growth of the Group of Seven (G-7) countries in the 1980s might have been, the adjustment coefficient α has been taken as 0.4. This implies that a country would aim to eliminate 40 percent of any excess deflationary gap in the first year and nearly 80 percent within three years. However, an absolute limit (of 2.0 percent of GNP) was placed on this term, on the reasoning that it is potentially dangerous to try to reduce excess capacity very fast. The one country that reduced its deflationary gap by more than 2 percent during a year in the period under review, the United States in 1984, saw its current account deficit explode by over 1.5 percent of GNP during that year.

Column 4 of each of the appendix tables A.1 through A.7 provides a rough quantification of the deflationary gap (d). This was constructed by first calculating the average rate of GNP growth over the period 1979–85. In

71

those countries where actual real growth exceeded 2.5 percent per year, namely Canada (2.7 percent) and Japan (4.2 percent), the actual rate of realized growth was taken to be the potential growth rate $\bar{g}$. In the other countries potential growth was set at 2.5 percent per year. The economy was then assumed to have been at full capacity at some point in the period, and the deflationary gap was measured as the shortfall of output below the full capacity level given by the growth of potential GNP from that level. (Thus, in the case of the United States, the economy was assumed to have been at full capacity at the end of 1979; given that output fell 0.2 percent in 1980, this implies that the deflationary gap at the end of that year was 2.7 percent.)

The major policy choice that has to be incorporated into the formula for demand growth is that of the priority to be given to reducing inflation. An aim of rapid disinflation would imply a low value for β, the proportion of inherited inflation that should be accommodated. The value of β was selected by examining the rate at which inflation was in fact squeezed down during 1981–85, a period generally considered to have been one of successful and rather rapid disinflation. During this period, most countries succeeded in reducing inflation by one-third in one year or another, but only Japan achieved a reduction of over 45 percent (and then only from a starting point of 1.8 percent inflation). It would make no sense to target a faster reduction in inflation than the economy could achieve, for that simply forces a recession. These facts suggest that a value of 0.7 would be reasonable for β.

The question also arises as to whether it is worth sacrificing output, even temporarily, to force inflation down to zero, especially as measured by the GNP deflator. Since stability of wholesale prices may well be consistent with an upward creep of the GNP deflator of as much as 2 percent per year, we decided to set $\hat{p}^*$, the acceptable or target inflation rate, at 2.

In order to reduce inflation on its intended path by $(1 - \beta)(\hat{p}_{t-1} - 2)$, it would be necessary to maintain an appropriate deflationary gap (d^*). What is appropriate in this context depends on the number of point-years of lost output needed to reduce inflation by 1 percent. Grubb, Jackman, and Layard (1982) estimated the unemployment cost of reducing inflation by 1 percent for OECD countries. Their individual country estimates seemed to vary too wildly to be plausible, but their overall average estimate suggested a need for 1.25 percent extra unemployment for one year. Since cyclical variations in output typically exceed those in unemployment, we adopted a uniform coefficient of two point-years of lost output as the cost of reducing inflation for all seven countries. This is somewhat less than typical estimates made in the early 1980s (figures of around 3), but seems broadly consistent with the deceleration of inflation achieved in the 1980s.

The purpose of the final term in the equation is to help the balance of payments adjustment process by making explicit the obligation of a country with an excessive current account surplus to expand domestic demand more rapidly than it wants its own output to grow. Similarly, a country with an excessive deficit should cut back the growth of demand below its planned rate of output growth so as to make room for the desired improvement in the balance of payments. One advantage of targeting the growth of domestic demand rather than nominal income would be to prevent a country that succeeds in growing by exporting more, when it already has an excessive surplus, from claiming that it had fulfilled its international obligations.

To calculate illustrative targets for the rate of growth of domestic demand, values must be selected for the parameter γ and the target current account balances, b^*. As far as γ is concerned, it was decided to take a value of 0.5, consistent with the standard assumption that adjustment of trade flows to exchange rate changes takes some two to three years.

In principle, the target values for b^* should be those used in calculating the target exchange rates, or fundamental equilibrium exchange rates (FEERs). But in fact our FEERs were based on calculations with current account targets for the years 1976–77, and the FEERs for those years were then updated in the light of major changes in the world economy. In some cases these were judged to have influenced current account targets, but no systematic effort has been made to update these. We plan to make such an effort in subsequent work, but it scarcely seems sensible to delay publication of the present study until that work is complete. We have therefore sought to allow for this uncertainty by taking a range for b^*, and allowing the term $(b_{t-1} - b^*)$ to take on nonzero values only when b_{t-1} exceeds the top of the range for b^* or falls below the bottom of the range.

The actual values assumed for the target ranges are shown in table A.8. For the four smaller countries that have not developed progressively larger imbalances through the 1980s, the ranges have been chosen around zero except during the years 1980–85 when temporarily high oil prices can be argued to have justified imbalances. For the three large countries, the ranges start off symmetrically but then move in the actual direction observed historically, to the maximum extent that we think might be sustainable.

Two other questions about the demand target merit mention. First, should the growth in nominal demand be made a rolling target, so that an overshoot in one year's target raises the base level for subsequent years, or should it take the form of a prespecified path? We have specified the form of a rolling target, for two reasons. One is political credibility: if inflation overshoots one year, no one will believe a promise to pull the price level back in subsequent years to where it would otherwise have been. Another is economic logic: we dislike inflation not primarily because it makes the price level y rather than x, but because the process of raising it from x to y distorts incentives and redistributes income. The damage would be compounded by pushing it back to x again.[1]

The other question is whether the coefficients α, β and γ should be the same for all countries, or whether they could differ among countries. As far as γ is concerned, one might argue that a common value is desirable in the interest of ensuring symmetry in the adjustment process and preventing the growth in global demand depending on the distribution of payments inbalances, although the facts that we have chosen a range for b^* and that the collective current account balance of the G-7 can vary imply that pressures will not necessarily be symmetrical anyway.

The case for imposition of uniform values of α and β seems even weaker. National variation in those parameters would, it is true, result in the growth of planned global demand depending on the international distribution of inflationary and deflationary pressures. On the other hand, the relative priority to be given to combating inflation and unemployment is a subject on which both political and national preferences can differ sharply, and an attempt to impose a uniform β could make the proposal unacceptable. The case therefore seems to be strong for allowing a measure of national discretion in choosing β. Our own calculations of hypothetical demand growth targets have nonetheless embodied a common value of 0.7.

After substituting this and the other parameters described above into equation (1), and rounding to one decimal place to avoid any suggestion of spurious accuracy, one derives the equation used to construct the target changes in demand shown in the final columns of tables A.1 through A.7:

$$\hat{y}_t^* = (1 + \bar{g}) + 0.5\hat{p}_{t-1} + \min.[0.4d_{t-1}, 2] + 0.5(b_{t-1} - b^*)/y.$$

---

1. This assumes an absence of contracts spanning the period from when the price level was initially x to when it might again be restored to the level x. If one judges that the difference between the strategies of minimizing future inflation and rolling back past inflation is likely to be significant only for time horizons of more than a year, "long" contracts are surely a small minority.

The formula was modified in two respects for 1980, in reflection of the second oil price increase. First, 3.5 percent was added to the inherited rates of inflation $\hat{p}_{t-1}$ for all seven countries, the figure being motivated by the estimates in the December 1979 *OECD Economic Outlook* that oil prices had increased by 66 percent and that each 10 percent increase added 0.5 percent to inflation. The basic assumption is, of course, that an oil price increase represents an exogenous shock to the inflation rate which should be worked down gradually, like any other inherited inflation. Second, the balance of payments adjustment term was suppressed where it was obvious that the oil price change could have been expected to produce the desired adjustment in the payments position anyway.

TABLE A.1   **United States: construction of targets for growth in domestic demand, 1980–87**

	(1)	(2)	(3)	(4)
Year	GNP growth *g* (percentage)	Increase in GNP deflator *p̂* (percentage)	Current account balance *b* (billion dollars)	Deflationary gap *d* (percentage)
1979	2.5	8.8	− 1.0	0.0
1980	− 0.2	9.0	1.8	2.7
1981	1.8	9.7	6.4	3.4
1982	− 2.5	6.4	− 9.1	8.4
1983	3.6	3.9	− 46.7	7.3
1984	6.5	3.9	− 106.5	3.3
1985	2.8	3.3	− 117.7	3.0
1986	2.5	2.7	− 140.6	3.0
1987	n.a.	n.a.	n.a.	n.a.

—   not applicable.
n.a.   not available.
Source: Columns 1–2, *OECD Economic Outlook* data base; column 3, IMF, *International*

TABLE A.2   **Japan: construction of targets for growth in domestic demand, 1980–87**

	(1)	(2)	(3)	(4)
Year	GNP growth *g* (percentage)	Increase in GNP deflator *p̂* (percentage)	Current account balance *b* (billion dollars)	Deflationary gap *d* (percentage)
1979	5.3	3.0	− 8.8	0.1
1980	4.3	3.8	− 10.8	0.0
1981	3.7	3.2	4.8	0.5
1982	3.1	1.8	6.9	1.6
1983	3.2	0.8	20.8	2.6
1984	5.1	1.2	35.0	1.7
1985	4.7	1.5	49.2	1.2
1986	2.5	1.8	86.0	3.0
1987	n.a.	n.a.	n.a.	n.a.

—   not applicable.
n.a.   not available.
Source: Columns 1–2, *OECD Economic Outlook* data base; column 3, IMF, *International*

(5)	(6)	(7)	(8)
Target reduction in deflationary gap min. [0.4 d_{t-1}, 2] (percentage)	Inflation allowance 0.5 $\hat{p}_{t-1}$ (percentage)	Target change in current account 0.5 $(b_{t-1} - b^*)/y$ (percentage of GNP)	Target change in demand $\hat{y}^*$ (percentage)
—	—	—	—
0.0	6.1[a]	0.0	9.7
1.1	4.5	0.0	9.1
1.3	4.8	0.0	9.6
2.0	3.2	0.0	8.7
2.0	1.9	−0.1	7.3
1.3	2.0	−0.8	6.0
1.2	1.7	−0.8	5.6
1.2	1.3	−1.0	5.0

Financial Statistics; column 8 is 3.5 plus the sum of columns 5, 6, and 7; see text for derivation of other columns.

a. 1979 inflation was increased by 3.5 percent to allow for the oil price shock.

(5)	(6)	(7)	(8)
Target reduction in deflationary gap min. [0.4 d_{t-1}, 2] (percentage)	Inflation allowance 0.5 $\hat{p}_{t-1}$ (percentage)	Target change in current account 0.5 $(b_{t-1} - b^*)/y$ (percentage of GNP)	Target change in demand $\hat{y}^*$ (percentage)
—	—	—	—
0.0	3.3[a]	−0.2	8.3
0.0	1.9	−0.3	6.8
0.2	1.6	0.0	7.0
0.7	0.9	0.0	6.8
1.0	0.4	0.0	6.6
0.7	0.6	0.1	6.6
0.5	0.8	0.5	6.9
1.2	0.9	1.6	8.9

Financial Statistics; column 8 is 5.2 plus the sum of columns 5, 6, and 7; see text for derivation of other columns.

a. 1979 inflation was increased by 3.5 percent to allow for the oil price shock.

T A B L E A.3   **Germany: construction of targets for growth in domestic demand, 1980–87**

	(1)	*(2)*	*(3)*	*(4)*
Year	*GNP growth* *g* *(percentage)*	*Increase in* *GNP deflator* *p̂* *(percentage)*	*Current account* *balance* *b* *(billion dollars)*	*Deflationary* *gap* *d* *(percentage)*
1979	4.0	4.0	− 6.2	0.0
1980	1.5	4.8	− 15.9	1.0
1981	0.0	4.0	− 5.0	3.5
1982	− 1.0	4.4	3.9	7.0
1983	1.9	3.2	4.2	7.6
1984	2.9	2.0	8.2	7.2
1985	2.4	2.2	15.7	7.3
1986	2.3	3.1	35.8	7.5
1987	n.a.	n.a.	n.a.	n.a.

—   not applicable.
n.a.   not available.
Source: Columns 1–2, *OECD Economic Outlook* data base; column 3, IMF, *International*

T A B L E A.4   **France: construction of targets for growth in domestic demand, 1980–87**

	(1)	*(2)*	*(3)*	*(4)*
Year	*GNP growth* *g* *(percentage)*	*Increase in* *GNP deflator* *p̂* *(percentage)*	*Current account* *balance* *b* *(billion dollars)*	*Deflationary* *gap* *d* *(percentage)*
1979	3.3	10.4	5.1	0.0
1980	1.0	12.2	− 4.2	1.5
1981	0.5	11.8	− 4.8	3.5
1982	1.8	12.6	− 12.1	4.2
1983	0.7	9.5	− 5.2	6.0
1984	1.5	7.2	− 0.9	6.9
1985	1.4	5.8	0.9	8.0
1986	2.0	5.3	0.4	8.5
1987	n.a.	n.a.	n.a.	n.a.

—   not applicable.
n.a.   not available.
Source: Columns 1–2, *OECD Economic Outlook* data base; column 3, IMF, *International*

(5)	(6)	(7)	(8)
		Target change in	
Target reduction	*Inflation*	*current account*	*Target change in*
in deflationary gap	*allowance*	*$0.5 (b_{t-1} - b^*)/y$*	*demand*
min. $[0.4 d_{t-1}, 2]$	*$0.5 \hat{p}_{t-1}$*	*(percentage of*	*$\hat{y}*$*
(percentage)	*(percentage)*	*GNP)*	*(percentage)*
—	—	—	—
0.0	3.8[a]	−0.1	7.2
0.4	2.4	−0.8	5.5
1.4	2.0	0.0	6.9
2.0	2.2	0.0	7.7
2.0	1.6	0.0	7.1
2.0	1.0	0.0	6.4
2.0	1.1	0.0	6.6
2.0	1.6	0.8	7.9

Financial Statistics; column 8 is 3.5 plus the sum of columns 5, 6, and 7; see text for derivation of other columns.

a. 1979 inflation was increased by 3.5 percent to allow for the oil price shock.

(5)	(6)	(7)	(8)
		Target change in	
Target reduction	*Inflation*	*current account*	*Target change in*
in deflationary gap	*allowance*	*$0.5 (b_{t-1} - b^*)/y$*	*demand*
min. $[0.4 d_{t-1}, 2]$	*$0.5 \hat{p}_{t-1}$*	*(percentage of*	*$\hat{y}*$*
(percentage)	*(percentage)*	*GNP)*	*(percentage)*
—	—	—	—
0.0	7.0[a]	0.0[b]	10.5
0.6	6.1	0.0	10.2
1.4	5.9	0.0	10.8
1.7	6.3	−0.4	11.1
2.0	4.8	0.0	10.2
2.0	3.6	0.0	9.1
2.0	2.9	0.0	8.4
2.0	2.7	0.0	8.2

Financial Statistics; column 8 is 3.5 plus the sum of columns 5, 6, and 7; see text for derivation of other columns.

a. 1979 inflation was increased by 3.5 percent to allow for the oil price shock.

b. Normal rule overridden because of deterioration in prospect from oil price increase.

TABLE A.5 **Italy: construction of targets for growth in domestic demand, 1980–87**

	(1)	(2)	(3)	(4)
Year	GNP growth g (percentage)	Increase in GNP deflator $\hat{p}$ (percentage)	Current account balance b (billion dollars)	Deflationary gap d (percentage)
1979	4.9	15.9	5.4	1.4
1980	3.9	20.6	−9.8	0.0
1981	0.2	18.3	−8.6	2.3
1982	−0.5	17.8	−5.7	5.3
1983	−0.2	14.9	0.5	8.0
1984	2.8	10.8	−2.8	7.7
1985	2.3	8.8	−4.0	7.9
1986	2.7	8.3	0.9	7.7
1987	n.a.	n.a.	n.a.	n.a.

— not applicable.
n.a. not available.
Source: Columns 1–2, *OECD Economic Outlook* data base; column 3, IMF, *International*

TABLE A.6 **United Kingdom: construction of targets for growth in domestic demand, 1980–87**

	(1)	(2)	(3)	(4)
Year	GNP growth g (percentage)	Increase in GNP deflator $\hat{p}$ (percentage)	Current account balance b (billion dollars)	Deflationary gap d (percentage)
1979	2.2	14.5	−1.4	0.0
1980	−2.5	19.8	7.5	5.0
1981	−1.3	11.5	13.1	8.8
1982	1.5	7.7	6.9	9.8
1983	3.3	5.1	4.7	8.0
1984	3.1	4.0	1.9	7.4
1985	3.5	6.1	5.3	6.4
1986	2.7	3.7	0.9	6.2
1987	n.a.	n.a.	n.a.	n.a.

— not applicable.
n.a. not available.
Source: Columns 1–2, *OECD Economic Outlook* data base; column 3, IMF, *International*

(5) Target reduction in deflationary gap min. $[0.4 \, d_{t-1}, 2]$ (percentage)	(6) Inflation allowance $0.5 \, \hat{p}_{t-1}$ (percentage)	(7) Target change in current account $0.5 \, (b_{t-1} - b^*)/y$ (percentage of GNP)	(8) Target change in demand $\hat{y}^*$ (percentage)
—	—	—	—
0.6	9.7[a]	0.0[b]	13.8
0.0	10.3	−0.2	13.6
0.9	9.2	−0.1	13.5
2.0	8.9	0.0	14.4
2.0	7.5	0.1	13.1
2.0	5.4	0.0	10.9
2.0	4.4	0.0	9.9
2.0	4.2	0.0	9.7

Financial Statistics; column 8 is 3.5 plus the sum of columns 5, 6, and 7; see text for derivation of other columns.

a. 1979 inflation was increased by 3.5 percent to allow for the oil price shock.

b. Normal rule overridden because of deterioration in prospect from oil price increase.

(5) Target reduction in deflationary gap min. $[0.4 \, d_{t-1}, 2]$ (percentage)	(6) Inflation allowance $0.5 \, \hat{p}_{t-1}$ (percentage)	(7) Target change in current account $0.5 \, (b_{t-1} - b^*)/y$ (percentage of GNP)	(8) Target change in demand $\hat{y}^*$ (percentage)
—	—	—	—
0.0	9.0[a]	0.0[b]	12.5
2.0	9.9	0.0	15.3
2.0	5.8	0.5	11.8
2.0	3.8	0.0	9.4
2.0	2.6	0.0	8.1
2.0	2.1	0.0	7.5
2.0	2.9	0.1	8.5
2.0	1.9	0.0	7.4

Financial Statistics; column 8 is 3.5 plus the sum of columns 5, 6, and 7; see text for derivation of other columns.

a. 1979 inflation was increased by 3.5 percent to allow for the oil price shock.

b. Normal rule overridden because of improvement in prospect from oil price increase.

TABLE A.7   **Canada: construction of targets for growth in domestic demand, 1980–87**

	(1)	(2)	(3)	(4)
Year	GNP growth g (percentage)	Increase in GNP deflator p̂ (percentage)	Current account balance b (billion dollars)	Deflationary gap d (percentage)
1979	3.2	12.2	−4.1	0.0
1980	1.5	10.5	−1.0	1.2
1981	3.7	10.8	−5.1	0.0
1982	−3.3	8.9	2.3	6.2
1983	3.1	4.9	2.4	5.3
1984	5.5	3.6	2.5	2.7
1985	4.0	3.4	−0.4	1.4
1986	3.2	2.8	−6.0	1.0
1987	n.a.	n.a.	n.a.	n.a.

—   not applicable.
n.a.   not available.
Source: Columns 1–2, *OECD Economic Outlook* data base; column 3, IMF, *International*

TABLE A.8   **Ranges of values assumed for target current account balances, b*** (billion dollars)

	United States		Japan		Germany		France	
Year	min.	max.	min.	max.	min.	max.	min.	max.
1979	−15	+15	−5	+5	−5	+5	−4	+4
1980	−20	+12	−5	+5	−5	+5	−8	0
1981	−25	+9	−5	+10	−5	+6	−8	0
1982	−30	+6	−5	+15	−5	+7	−8	0
1983	−35	+3	−5	+20	−4	+8	−8	0
1984	−40	0	−5	+25	−3	+9	−8	0
1985	−45	0	−5	+30	−2	+10	−8	0
1986	−50	0	0	+35	0	+20	−4	+4

Source: See text.

(5) Target reduction in deflationary gap min. $[0.4\ d_{t-1}, 2]$ (percentage)	(6) Inflation allowance $0.5\ \hat{p}_{t-1}$ (percentage)	(7) Target change in current account $0.5\ (b_{t-1} - b^*)/y$ (percentage of GNP)	(8) Target change in demand $\hat{y}^*$ (percentage)
—	—	—	—
0.0	7.9[a]	0.0[b]	11.6
0.5	5.3	0.0	9.5
0.0	5.4	−0.3	8.8
2.0	4.5	0.0	10.2
2.0	2.5	0.0	8.2
1.1	1.8	0.0	6.6
0.6	1.7	0.0	6.0
0.4	1.4	−1.0	4.5

Financial Statistics; column 8 is 3.7 plus the sum of columns 5, 6, and 7; see text for derivation of other columns.

a. 1979 inflation was increased by 3.5 percent because of oil price increase.

b. Normal rule overridden because of improvement in prospect from oil price increases.

Italy		United Kingdom		Canada	
min.	max.	min.	max.	min.	max.
−4	+4	−4	+4	−3	+3
−8	0	0	+8	−3	+3
−8	0	0	+8	−3	+3
−8	0	0	+8	−3	+3
−8	0	0	+8	−3	+3
−8	0	0	+8	−3	+3
−8	0	0	+8	−3	+3
−4	+4	−4	+4	−3	+3

Appendix B   On the Design of Policy Rules

The blueprint presented in this study involves assigning policy instruments to the pursuit of chosen intermediate targets by feedback rules (which adjust the instruments as and when deviations from these targets occur). Neither the assignment of instruments nor the feedback rules themselves have been based on explicit optimal control techniques, however. In this respect, our approach differs from much of the recent literature on international macro-economic policy coordination which assumes optimization—by each country separately or by a set of countries acting cooperatively.

In this appendix we pursue a number of more-or-less technical issues raised by our approach. First, why should any government choose to adhere to a policy regime such as that proposed here, rather than pursuing a course of individual policy optimization? Second, how can the feedback rules be designed so as to be robust to misspecification? Third, how does the policy regime described by the blueprint compare with the alternatives—with free floating with monetary targets, for example, or with a return to fixed exchange rates? And, last of all, what are the implications of genuine intellectual differences among participating governments about how the world works for the design of such a regime?

Policy Regimes

The basic reasons for advocating a policy regime, rather than leaving each country free to optimize separately, are twofold—the presence of *externalities* in international economic relationships at any point of time, and the problem of *time consistency* in relationships over time.

Where there are significant externalities, then cooperative rules can be found which dominate individual optimization that ignores such externalities (e.g., "Don't litter"). Indeed, recent game theory has shown that such cooperative behavior can be sustained as individually rational in the context of a repeated game where bad behavior on previous occasions can be punished

84

in later phases of the game. That is to stay, sticking to a cooperative rule can be made *individually* rational if departure from it is punished.

To cope with externalities by cooperative rules of behavior is not enough, however. There is a separate argument for "rules rather than discretion," developed by Kydland and Prescott (1977). The proposition is that, in an intertemporal context, unconstrained optimization is inefficient relative to outcomes that are obtainable by *precommitment*. For example, money supply targets provide a way of avoiding the inflationary expectations that may arise under a regime of pure discretion. Precommitment is in principle a solution to the inefficiency of discretionary (or "time consistent") policy. And once again, the possibility that agents may be punished later (by loss of reputation, or whatever) for departures from rule-governed behavior may also sustain outcomes which are preferable to unconstrained individual optimization.

In a recent article, Rogoff (1985) showed that efforts to solve the problem of externalities by explicit coordination may exacerbate the "time consistency" problem (if the coordinated government is free to use its own unlimited discretion). Specifically, he showed that international monetary cooperation could be counterproductive if it exacerbated the credibility problem of central banks vis-à-vis the private sector. Coordinated monetary expansion yields a better output-inflation trade-off than unilateral expansion because it does not induce a depreciation of the currency. If wage-setters realize that the incentive to inflate is higher in a cooperative regime, they will demand higher nominal wage increases, thus worsening the output-inflation trade-off. On the other hand, a cooperative response to supply disturbances is mutually beneficial in his model.

A *policy regime* emerges as a solution to both problems identified here. Adherence to such a regime only becomes individually rational when "punishments" of some sort are involved. But the essential basis for such a regime lies in the superiority of rules over discretion in the presence of externalities and of the need for intertemporal precommitment.

In principle, given international agreement on an economic model and on policy coordination, together with the power to precommit, the technique of policy optimization may be used to determine the sort of rules such a regime might adopt. In the absence of such a detailed consensus—and in the belief that simple rules will be much more comprehensible and therefore easier to implement—we have chosen to adopt the more familiar approach of assigning the instruments of monetary and fiscal policy to external and internal objectives.

Robustness

In Edison, Miller, and Williamson (1987) we constructed a small analytical model of a two-country world economy to check the viability of the policy rules of the blueprint by a set of deterministic simulations (using assumed values for the coefficients). It was established that the proposed rules lead both economies to converge on zero inflation after an inflationary shock despite the absence of either of the traditional "nominal anchors" that have been assumed to be necessary to ensure this, namely a constant nominal exchange rate (in a world of foreign price stability) or a constant growth rate of the money supply. And this occurs despite the incorporation of a real exchange rate rule, which analysts using simple models have argued to be a recipe for loss of control over inflation (Adams and Gros 1986). The reason is that our system incorporates a nominal income target (with only partial accommodation of inflation) and an obligation to direct fiscal policy to the pursuit of that target.

In that paper the intermediate targets were pursued by feedback rules which incorporated both "proportional" and "integral" correction terms. For example, the "error correction" rule for setting world interest rates, r_a, is of the form:

$$r_a = c_p e_a + c_i \int_{-\infty}^{t} e_a(s)ds$$

where the error, e_a, is the percentage shortfall of world nominal income below its target trajectory, and c_p and c_i are the (negative) coefficients of response (to the current error and to the integral of past errors respectively).

We believe it is important for policy feedback rules to include both terms— as Phillips argued in his classic paper of 1954. Indeed, even when it might appear that proportional control is good enough, integral terms can play an important role if the model being used is misspecified—as Rosenbrock and McMorran (1971) and Salmon and Young (1979) have pointed out.

A typical example of the need for both types of control is provided by the problem of securing "optimal" disinflation in a closed economy where core inflation evolves adaptively. Assume specifically that one chooses y (output) so as to minimize a cost function of the form

$$\int_{t}^{\infty} [(y(s)-y^*)^2 + b^2 z^2(s)]ds$$

where it is believed that y^* is the stable-inflation level of output, and

$$Dp = f(y - y^*) + z$$
$$Dz = g(Dp - z)$$

where Dp denotes inflation and z core inflation. The *optimal control rule* here (see, for example, Miller 1985) is simply

$$y - y^* = -bz,$$

that is, to reduce output below y^* when core inflation is positive (and vice versa), the coefficient of response reflecting the weight attached to core inflation in the cost function.

Such a feedback rule, where the strength of policy action is *proportional* to the deviation of core inflation from its target rate (zero), is indeed optimal given that f, g, and y^* are correctly known. But suppose that the authorities have been over-optimistic about the NAIRU, and the output level at which inflation stabilizes is not y^* but $y^* - x$, so that the inflation equation above should actually be

$$Dp = f(y - y^* + x) + z.$$

Though use of the ''optimal'' rule in this case would lead the economy to the correct stable-inflation rate of output, it will result in a steady-state rate of inflation (of x/b). This steady-state rate of inflation can, however, be eliminated if the proportional term were augmented by an *integral* term to give a revised rule

$$y - y^* = -bz - c \int_{-\infty}^{t} z(s)ds.$$

In this case output can be kept at the revised natural rate ($y^* - x$) *without* persistent inflation, when the integral of past core inflation builds up to x/c.

The idea that one should respond to the integral of past errors is probably most familiar to economists in the international monetary field from the work of Robert Mundell (see, for example, 1968, ch. 14). Recognizing that the authorities may not know where equilibrium is, he proposed that they should adjust their policy instruments according to a rule of the form

$$Dr_a = ce_a.$$

As may be seen by integrating, such a rule is a pure integral correction mechanism, that is, it incorporates just the second term of our expression.

Provided that instruments are correctly assigned to targets (that the Principle of Effective Market Classification is followed, in Mundell's terminology), such a rule should lead ultimately to equilibrium. But it nonetheless has an important disadvantage, namely that it leads to highly cyclical behavior on the path to equilibrium.

Where one has some, but not perfect, knowledge of equilibrium values and model structure, it seems reasonable to suppose that performance may be improved by including both forms of correction (as in our 1987 paper), with proportional correction pushing the system toward what is believed to be equilibrium and the integral term providing a safeguard against getting the estimate wrong. It may be possible to get further insights by policy-evaluation exercises on global econometric models (as in Bryant et al.) to see whether one can get a system that is both reasonably efficient and also robust.

Consistency with a range of expectations-formation mechanisms is another important requirement for robustness. Consistency with rational expectations—with the hypothesis that it is impossible to fool the public systematically, since they will learn from experience and make the best use of available information in forming their expectations—is a minimal test of a policy regime. We see no reason for contending that this test is not satisfied by our proposal. Indeed, we believe that our proposal will work better if expectations are rational, for this will ensure that the announced exchange rate target will provide a stabilizing focus for expectations as long as the FEER is chosen on the basis of the best available information. And, at least according to some theories, it will also help ensure that the rate of inflation does indeed decline along its intended path and without a higher-than-expected cost in terms of unemployment. But a policy regime should not *depend* upon expectations being rational in order to function satisfactorily, for as noted in the study it seems difficult to understand some recent incidents in the foreign exchange market except on the basis of extrapolative expectations.

Comparing International Regimes

In a second exercise (Miller and Williamson 1987), we have analyzed the effects of various policy regimes—including that in our blueprint—on the long run (asymptotic) variances of output, prices, and the balance of payments when the economic system is subject to stochastic disturbances. Three regimes were examined: free floating with money supply targets, McKinnon's proposal for global monetary coordination under fixed exchange rates, and the extended target zone system proposed in the blueprint. (It should, however, be noted that for this comparative study three simplifying assumptions were made: first, that the nominal targets were exogenously determined, rather than being rebased to accommodate past inflation and current unemployment; second, that only proportional responses were used in all regimes; and, third, that the real exchange rate was kept at the middle of the band.)

Using the formulae in Miller and Williamson (with the parameter values $\gamma = \phi = \sigma = \delta = 0.5$, $\eta = 0.1$, $k = 1$, and $\theta = 0.93$), one can calculate asymptotic variances in response to supply-side shocks to the inflation equation, for example, as summarized in the upper part of table B.1. There the asymptotic variance of the price level is given in the top row and of output in the second row (as a multiple of the variance of the shocks in both cases).

It can be seen that, for these supply-side shocks, the product of the first and second rows comes to unity: the regimes are "trading off" variations in prices and output. The first two columns show the effects of global shocks to global prices and output; the remaining three show the effects of country-specific shocks to international price and output *differences*. (Since the *level* of output and prices in either country can be obtained as the weighted sum of the global and difference variables, the *variance* of national output and prices may be found by appropriately combining the variables shown in the table—with weights of 1 and 0.25 on the global and differential variances respectively.)

In the first column one can see that for both a world money supply target as originally proposed by McKinnon and for a global nominal income target as proposed in our blueprint (pursued with an equally active use of interest rates), the variance of prices is likely to exceed that of output. (If one were to include shocks to the velocity of money as well, they would increase the variances associated with the money supply rule, leaving those for the nominal income target unchanged.)

Targeting the price level directly, as McKinnon has more recently recommended, does reduce price variance, as one might expect (see column 2), but at the cost of higher output variance.

Turning now to the country-specific inflation shocks, one sees, in columns 3 and 4, that the fluctuations in relative prices and of relative output levels are much closer together. The reason is that, in an open economy, the movement of the real exchange rate adds an extra channel to monetary policy.

TABLE B.1   **Long-run variances of prices and output under different regimes**

	Global Economy		Inter-country differences		
	Money and nominal income targets	*Price level target*	*Floating with money targets*	*McKinnon's proposal*	*Blueprint*
(a) *Supply-side shocks*					
Variance of prices	3.6	2.6	0.93	0.85	3.2
Variance of output	0.28	0.38	1.07	1.18	0.31
(b) *Demand shocks*					
Variance of prices	1.11	1.54	0.19	0.29	0.31
Variance of output	1.32	2.59	1.05	1.78	0.42

In addition to the direct effect of real interest rates on aggregate demand, the real interest rate will influence the trade balance via its effect on the real exchange rate. Interestingly, however, the "gold standard" results appearing in column 4—where the country with high inflation sticks to a fixed exchange rate and suffers a loss in competitiveness—are much the same as those for free floating with money supply targets (in column 3). The intuitive reason for this is that if, as here, the exchange rate does not significantly "overshoot" under floating, and if the money target is constant, then the floating nominal exchange rate will be pretty stable too.[1]

Under both these two regimes international competitiveness will fluctuate as relative prices move but the nominal exchange rate remains stable. As can be seen from the last column, moving nominal rates so as to keep

---

1. Floating exchange rates have not in fact proven stable, and this instability cannot be ascribed solely to uncertainty about macroeconomic policy. In the paper referred to we therefore include "fads" in the foreign exchange market which affect the behavior of the floating exchange rate, but disappear when the exchange rate is fixed or managed. Such fads increase the variance associated with floating rates relative to the alternative regimes.

competitiveness constant does stabilize output, but it means that prices become more volatile (as found by Dornbusch in Williamson 1981). The outcomes begin to look more like those for the closed economy—which makes sense as the monetary authorities are acting so as to prevent real exchange rates from moving as they have in the previous two cases.

What happens to the trade balance in these various regimes? Under the stylized version of the blueprint, competitiveness is constant—which helps to stabilize trade: under the other two regimes competitiveness varies a lot (which increases fluctuations in trade), but this is offset in part by the positive correlation between competitiveness and output. On balance, for the parameters used here, trade fluctuates considerably more for the freely floating and for the fixed nominal exchange rate regimes than for the managed exchange rate system.

In the lower half of table B.1 the asymptotic variances arising from stochastic shifts in demand are also shown. For these shocks, the product of price and output variances is no longer constant across regimes. For global increases and decreases in aggregate demand, for example, both of these variances rise under a price level target relative to those prevailing with money supply or nominal income targeting. The reason for this is that money supply and money income targets cause a prompt stabilizing response to a shift of real output, but the price target only responds later, when the output shift has caused inflation.

For country-specific demand shocks (that is, shifts of demand from one country to the other), the *national* nominal income targets of the blueprint keep the variance of both output and prices at a low level in much the same way as did the global nominal income target (except that here it is fiscal policy that adjusts, not interest rates). Where the rate is floating, the adjustment takes the form of movements of real exchange rates, which help to stabilize prices and to some extent output. Under fixed exchange rates, however, there is no prompt response to counter the demand shift, and the output variance is the highest of the three regimes.

The stochastic results just described involve an exogenous setting for the nominal targets, with no base drift, so the variance of the price level is bounded even in the long run. In the blueprint, however, it is proposed that the nominal income target respond *endogenously* to the state of the economy— accommodating part of recent inflation, easing when the economy is in recession, etc. As any given disturbance to the price level will no longer be ultimately reversed, the long-run variance of the price level is not bounded.

The asymptotic variance of inflation may still remain bounded, however, as is noted in a footnote to the text.

This idea, that one can stabilize inflation without necessarily tying down the price *level*, is most commonly associated with the name of Wicksell, who noted that his policy recommendations left the price level in a "neutral" equilibrium. (A physical analogy for this neutral equilibrium might be a foam rubber ball lying in thick sludge in the guttering of a roof of infinite length. Random gusts of wind will move it back and forth, so in time it can wander anywhere along the gutter. But the *rate of change* of its position will remain bounded.) As against this view, it is perhaps the monetarists (following Walras rather than Wicksell) who have been most prominent in arguing that in principle control of inflation needs an exogenously fixed nominal anchor— in the form of a fixed money supply target. In practice, however, they too have been prepared to allow for "base drift" (US) or "rebasing the monetary targets" (United Kingdom) to accommodate past overshooting. If this rebasing is regular it means that the asymptotic variance of the price level (but not the inflation rate) will also tend to infinity under their proposals.

The point can be established formally as follows. Consider a Phillips curve augmented by core inflation which is formed adaptively, namely

(1) $Dp = fy + z + u,$

where u is a random error (zero-mean, white Gaussian noise), and

(2) $Dz = g(Dp - z)$

where y is output measured from the "natural rate," p is the log of prices, z is core inflation and Dp is therefore current inflation. This formulation generates tremendous persistence in inflation (since z, a moving average of past inflation, has a one-for-one effect on current inflation). Nevertheless, *strict* control of money income, like a fixed quantity of money under the quantity theory, can stabilize the price level—if it is unyielding.

To see this, let $Dp + Dy = 0$, which implies

(3) $p = -y + k,$

where k is set equal to zero by choice of units. Substituting (2) and (3) into (1) yields the system

(4) $\begin{bmatrix} Dp \\ Dz \end{bmatrix} = \begin{bmatrix} -f & 1 \\ -gf & 0 \end{bmatrix} \begin{bmatrix} p \\ z \end{bmatrix} + \begin{bmatrix} 1 \\ g \end{bmatrix} u \equiv A \begin{bmatrix} p \\ z \end{bmatrix} + Bu.$

Since the matrix denoted A is stable (it has two roots with negative real parts), one can determine the asymptotic variance-covariance matrix for p and z, denoted by V and defined by the formula

$$AV + V^t A^t = -BQB^t$$

where Q is the variance of the zero-mean random error in (4), and t denotes transposition. As exogenously set nominal targets ensure that the price level constantly returns to a predetermined level, so they ensure that the long run (or asymptotic) distribution of the price level has a bounded variance.

But this is no longer true if the growth of nominal income, or of the money supply, becomes endogenous as a result of "rebasing." Specifically, let

(5) $Dy + Dp = -ay + bz$

so, by substitution from (1),

(6) $Dy = -(a+f)y - (1-b)z - u.$

Collecting the equations together now yields the system

$$(7) \quad \begin{bmatrix} Dp \\ Dz \\ Dy \end{bmatrix} = \begin{bmatrix} 0 & 1 & f \\ 0 & 0 & fg \\ 0 & -(1-b) & -(a+f) \end{bmatrix} \begin{bmatrix} p \\ z \\ y \end{bmatrix} + \begin{bmatrix} 1 \\ g \\ -1 \end{bmatrix} = A \begin{bmatrix} p \\ z \\ y \end{bmatrix} + Bu.$$

Notice that the first column of A is zero, so one root must be zero. The presence of a zero root means that there is "hysteresis" in the price level—it will be left permanently changed by temporary shocks. As p is the simple sum of past values of y, z and u, its asymptotic variance is infinite.

Notice, however, that the remaining two variables, core inflation and output, form a well-behaved subsystem, namely:

$$(8) \quad \begin{bmatrix} Dz \\ Dy \end{bmatrix} = \begin{bmatrix} 0 & fg \\ -(1-b) & -(a+f) \end{bmatrix} \begin{bmatrix} z \\ y \end{bmatrix} + \begin{bmatrix} g \\ -1 \end{bmatrix} u$$

which has stable roots and so a finite asymptotic variance-covariance matrix; which was what was to be shown.

The basic Wicksellian idea which these equations are designed to demonstrate is that the price level (being the simple sum of *all past inflation*) may tend to wander without limit under the impact of stochastic shocks, even when a measure of inflation—*recent* changes of prices only—is being kept under reasonable control.

Intellectual Differences

No system of guidelines for securing internationally consistent macroeconomic policies is likely to be acceptable if there exist sufficiently profound differences in views on how the economy works among countries. If, for example, some countries accept the (Keynesian) thesis that a bigger budget deficit expands demand while others believe that it contracts demand, then they are hardly likely to agree on a set of rules whose design embodies a particular answer to that question. It is conceivable that present differences are so great as to preclude agreement. We are sufficiently eclectic to believe that most views contain an element of truth and therefore that a careful distinction between circumstances where different relations hold sway may be able to bridge apparent differences of view.

For example, it is important to achieve adequate levels of national savings and to avoid excessive indebtedness on the part of the public sector, and there *are* even circumstances in which an increased budget deficit can be counterproductive from the standpoint of expanding demand. It is surely possible that recognizing these facts and building them into the medium-term objectives may help to make the Keynesian fiscal policy embodied in rule (C) acceptable to those who have traditionally regarded themselves as "anti-Keynesian."

If differences of view on how the economy works turns out to be irreconcilable, that does not dispose of the *need* for policy coordination; it will just make it more difficult to achieve. Coordination will have to be organized in a quite different way, as a series of ad hoc bargains that all parties perceive as being in their short-run interest.[2] It seems highly unlikely that a series of ad hoc bargains will be capable of generating such continuous cooperation as an agreed set of policy guidelines would. The reason is

---

2. It would thus be much closer to the situation modeled in most of the academic literature on policy coordination, for example Buiter and Marston (1985). A few papers in this literature seek, as we do, to provide rules of thumb for benign but puzzled policymakers, but most of them enquire instead into the possibility of mutually beneficial bargains between policymakers wholly dedicated to the pursuit of national self-interest and with total understanding of how the economy works. Admittedly there is still a difference between the problem posed in these models and the situation envisaged in the text, in that failure to agree in these models stems from conflicting national interests rather than conflicting visions of how the economy works, a topic explored by Frankel in Bryant et al. (forthcoming).

fundamental: the latter embrace the possibility of intertemporal trade-offs—country A modifying its policy today even though it sees no particular gain from doing so except the expectation that country B will do the same under analogous future circumstances—whereas the former requires each bargain to benefit each country at the time.

It is possible that there may in fact be some benefit in a situation in which, while not unbridgeable, the world views of the various parties involved do differ quite substantially. This will make it more difficult to agree on a set of rules, but the countervailing benefit, given genuine uncertainty about the nature of the world, is the greater likelihood that any agreed set of rules would still be likely to bring mutual gain under a wide range of circumstances.[3] In other words, rules are unlikely to win acceptance unless they are indeed robust.

---

3. For the same reason, it would be silly to appoint an advisory panel of economists who were all dedicated Keynesians, monetarists, or supply-siders: the best assurance of useful advice comes from choosing a panel with a common commitment to intellectual honesty but a diversity of views.

Appendix C A Simulation Study of Target Zones

The multicountry model (MCM) is a linked system of five quarterly national macroeconometric models, for the United States, Canada, Japan, Germany, and the United Kingdom, with an abbreviated residual sector covering the rest of the world. The individual models vary in size from 150 to 250 behavioral equations and identities. The country models are linked to each other by equations modeling bilateral trade in goods, trade in services, investment income flows, and exchange rates.

The prototype model is in many ways a conventional Keynesian macro-economic model. There are four domestic agents: consumers, firms, commercial banks, and the government (fiscal and monetary authorities). There are four markets in the model: domestic output, labor, money, and bonds. Nominal wages are sticky, so that the amount of labor employed is variable, and output can adjust to meet aggregate demand. The aggregate supply curve is given by producers, who set prices at a markup over variable cost. In contrast to the goods market, asset markets are perfectly competitive, and agents are assumed to be risk neutral. There is only one nominal interest rate—short- and long-term securities are assumed to be perfect substitutes. Foreign and home currency bonds are also assumed to be perfect substitutes, so that open interest parity holds in the foreign exchange market. Expectations about future variables are adaptive. The penultimate version of the model is described in detail in Stevens et al. (1984), and the latest version is outlined in Edison, Marquez and Tryon (1986).

AUTHORS' NOTE: *It is mentioned at the beginning of section 3 that, in conjunction with Hali Edison, we undertook a simulation study on the Fed's MCM of how target zones might have operated over the period 1976–85. This appendix reproduces, with minimal modifications to make it self-contained, section 2 of Edison, Miller, and Williamson (1987), which presented that study.*

EXPERIMENTAL DESIGN

The question that we posed to the MCM was how economic outcomes with respect to output, inflation, interest rates, and exchange rates would have differed in the five countries had a monetary reaction function of the form of (1), below, been superimposed on the actual history of the period 1976:Q1 to 1985:Q4:

(1) $\Delta r = f(c - \bar{c}), f' < 0,$

where Δr is the policy adjustment in the interest rate, $c = \log EP/P^*$ is the real effective exchange rate, which measures the level of competitiveness (with E being measured in units of foreign exchange per unit of national currency so that a decrease in c signifies greater competitiveness), and $\bar{c}$ is the target level of competitiveness or what Williamson (1985) christened the "fundamental equilibrium exchange rate" (FEER).

To evaluate this, we took historical values as the baseline and reran the model under the assumption that the monetary authorities had started adjusting interest rates from their historical levels according to a reaction function in the class of (1) at the start of 1976.

Since the MCM does not contain effective exchange rates, the first step was to construct an index for the real effective exchange rate of each of the five countries in the model. The indices chosen were trade-weighted averages of the bilateral exchange rates against each of the four other currencies explicitly modeled in the MCM. These indices show significantly more variability than conventional, broader EER indices, especially for Germany (whose EER is in the real world stabilized by the large proportion of German trade conducted with other European countries that are not modeled by the MCM but maintain rather stable exchange rates against the deutsche mark).

The second step was to incorporate the policy reaction functions into the five country models. We selected the cubic form:

(2) $r = r_b - [(c - \bar{c})/n]^3$

where r is the three-month Treasury bill rate, r_b is the baseline level of the interest rate, c is the index of the real effective exchange rate described above, $\bar{c}$ is the target level of competitiveness, and n is half the width of the target zone. The target REER, $\bar{c}$, was selected by placing the four-country index of c the same percentage above or below $\bar{c}$ in 1976:Q4 as Williamson's (1985) composite REER was above or below his estimated FEER in that quarter. Changes in $\bar{c}$ in other periods tracked Williamson's estimates of changes in the FEERs.[1]

The essence of the policy reaction function (2) is that the monetary authorities are assumed to have adjusted interest rates whenever the REER deviated from the center of the zone. However, the adjustment is rather small when the exchange rate lies within the target zone since $(c - \bar{c})/n$ is less than one. The adjustment increases rapidly once the exchange rate leaves the zone.

The principal advantage of the formulation in (2) is that it allows r to be a continuous function of the misalignment $(c - \bar{c})$.[2] But it also has several other advantages. A country does not have an absolute obligation to keep the rate within the target zone ("soft buffers"). Moreover, as the currency approaches or leaves the target zone, the monetary authorities increasingly act to bring the exchange rate back toward its target, but their action is not abrupt. Finally, if two or more countries go out of the zone, then both or all of the countries change their policy.

From an operational standpoint, the implementation of this monetary policy requires switching the rule off in the baseline and allowing the model to solve interest rates as they are normally modelled in the MCM. (Each country has its own treasury bill interest rate equation.) During the policy simulation the original equation is switched off and only the reaction function described above is in effect.

SIMULATION RESULTS

Figure C.1 and table C.1 summarize the results of this simulation. Each graph gives the target zone bands, the actual path of the real effective exchange rate (using the trade-weighted basket of the four other MCM

---

1. Figure C.1 shows the resulting target zones. Note that these were constructed by linear interpolation between the dates for which Williamson had attempted to estimate FEERs, namely the 1976–77 average, 1983:Q1, and 1984:Q4 for the four major countries. For Canada estimates were made only for 1984 and 1985 (Williamson in Wonnacott 1987), and the 1984 zone was carried back unchanged to 1976. Clearly these procedures are somewhat crude and actual target zones calculated ex ante would doubtless have been somewhat different, but they surely capture the spirit of the proposal better than taking ex post averages as the center of the target zones.
2. We encountered nonconvergence in the simulations when we made the policy reaction function discontinuous.

FIGURE C.1   **Real effective exchange rates and target zones**

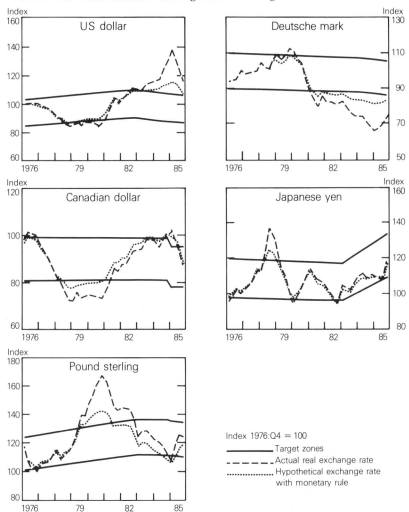

Index 1976:Q4 = 100
——— Target zones
- - - - Actual real exchange rate
·············· Hypothetical exchange rate
with monetary rule

TABLE C.1   **Impact of target zones on key variables**

	1976	1977	1978	1979
United States				
Real GNP (percentage)	0.1	0.2	0.0	−0.7
Price level (percentage)	0.0	0.1	0.0	−0.1
Interest rate (percentage points)	−0.2	−0.0	0.6	0.9
Real exchange rate (percentage)	−0.9	−0.3	1.6	2.3
Current balance (billion dollars)	0.1	0.4	0.1	−1.5
Canada				
Real GNP (percentage)	0.2	0.4	−0.0	−1.5
Price level (percentage)	0.4	0.2	−0.4	−1.4
Interest rate (percentage points)	−0.7	0.0	1.6	2.4
Real exchange rate (percentage)	−2.0	−0.6	3.9	6.7
Current balance (billion dollars)	−0.2	−0.0	0.5	0.9
Germany				
Real GNP (percentage)	0.0	−0.1	−0.1	0.2
Price level (percentage)	−0.1	−0.1	0.2	0.7
Interest rate (percentage points)	0.1	0.0	−0.1	−0.4
Real exchange rate (percentage)	0.2	0.1	−0.3	−2.6
Current balance (billion dollars)	0.2	−0.1	−1.6	−0.8
Japan				
Real GNP (percentage)	−0.2	−0.6	−0.2	1.4
Price level (percentage)	−0.1	−0.1	0.1	−0.0
Interest rate (percentage points)	0.5	0.0	−1.5	−0.1
Real exchange rate (percentage)	1.5	0.0	−5.0	−1.3
Current balance (billion dollars)	−0.0	−0.6	−1.5	4.3
United Kingdom				
Real GNP (percentage)	−0.0	−0.3	−0.4	0.1
Price level (percentage)	−0.4	−0.4	−0.2	0.8
Interest rate (percentage points)	0.4	0.2	0.1	−0.8
Real exchange rate (percentage)	0.9	0.8	0.7	−2.9
Current balance (billion dollars)	0.6	−0.2	−0.5	−1.7

Note: Amounts shown are deviations from the baseline path.
Source: MCM.

1980	1981	1982	1983	1984	1985
−1.5	−1.7	−1.5	−0.6	0.6	2.5
−0.3	−0.8	−1.1	−1.5	−1.7	−1.3
0.6	−0.0	−0.4	−0.9	−2.5	−3.3
4.7	2.3	−0.6	−2.5	−8.1	−11.4
−2.5	−4.1	−3.3	−2.3	−4.1	−2.7
−2.6	−2.7	−2.5	−1.9	−1.3	−0.9
−2.3	−3.4	−5.0	−6.9	−9.4	−11.6
1.6	0.3	−0.1	−0.6	−0.8	−1.3
8.1	4.8	3.0	1.9	1.1	0.2
1.5	1.3	1.6	2.4	4.1	4.1
0.4	0.1	−0.7	−1.4	−2.4	−3.7
0.8	−0.3	−0.7	−1.5	−3.5	−5.1
−0.2	1.7	2.0	2.8	4.4	4.2
−1.1	4.4	5.8	9.2	15.6	18.4
0.5	2.0	2.2	2.5	5.9	−0.8
1.7	1.4	1.0	0.2	−0.4	−1.7
0.3	0.5	0.6	0.8	0.6	0.5
0.3	−0.0	0.7	0.2	0.2	0.4
1.2	−1.3	−0.2	−1.7	−1.9	−0.1
−1.9	−0.9	0.7	−1.7	2.4	−3.5
1.7	4.0	3.5	2.8	2.5	1.7
4.1	5.4	6.4	8.7	10.6	12.2
−3.8	−1.9	−0.3	0.2	1.3	1.3
−11.2	−10.4	−7.9	−7.0	−5.6	−5.0
−5.6	0.6	0.1	0.0	1.3	2.0

currencies), and the path of the simulated real effective rate for each country. The table reports the impact on five key economic variables, in the form of the difference in the annual average for each variable between the simulation and the baseline. Note that real exchange rates are being presented in the form familiar to Anglo-Saxon readers, so that an increase signifies a real appreciation of the domestic currency, and a loss of competitiveness.

Several features of the results merit comment. The first and most obvious is that rule (2) does indeed succeed in appreciably diminishing the magnitude of misalignments. In retrospect the rule might have been made somewhat stronger. The interest rate changes needed to secure the reduction in misalignments turn out to be distinctly modest, according to the MCM, so that a strengthening in the reaction function should be acceptable. Moreover, for two reasons, the MCM may well underestimate the impact of a target zone system on exchange rates. One is that it neglects intervention and jawboning and assumes that interest-rate changes are the only instrument for influencing exchange rates. The other is that it neglects the impact that exchange rate targeting might have had in focusing market expectations and thus limiting misalignments caused by speculative bubbles. Interpretation should bear in mind that both our rule and the effects of having a rule are on the weak side.

A second observation is that the simulation does not suggest that a loosening of US monetary policy with the aim of limiting the dollar's overvaluation from 1983 on would have substantially increased inflation. On the contrary, the US price level is actually slightly *lower* under the target zone simulation than in the baseline. This is because the lower GNP resulting from higher interest rates and a higher dollar in the years of dollar undervaluation (1978–80) did more to push inflation down than the lower interest rates and dollar from 1983 on pushed inflation up. But the results for the United Kingdom suggest that it would be unwise to dismiss the fears that real exchange rate targeting could undermine anti-inflation policy: it may merely be that these effects come with rather long lags.

A third observation is that the impact on current balances is derisory, or even perverse. According to the MCM, Japan's current surplus would have been only $3 billion smaller in 1985, while the current deficit of the United States would actually have been $3 billion *larger*. (Admittedly, the deficit would have declined by an annual rate of $4 billion by the last quarter of 1985, when the simulation ended.) One reason for the modest size of these changes is the J-curve. But another and more important reason is income effects: the lower dollar and interest rates expand US real GNP and therefore suck in more imports.

It seems, therefore, that a target zone system may require the complementary use of fiscal policy if it is to yield satisfactory results. To test this hypothesis, we undertook a second simulation in which the monetary rule (2) was supplemented by a compensatory fiscal policy which held real GNP at its baseline level. The results are shown in table C.2. (We do not show a second set of figures for the impact on exchange rates, since these are very similar to those in figure C.1.)

Inspection of table C.2 suggests the importance of supplementing an exchange rate-oriented monetary policy with a complementary fiscal policy. Inflation in the UK is now only modestly higher than in the baseline, and even that is true only until 1982; by 1985 the price *level* is only 3 percent higher. Moreover, it is now clear that exchange rate adjustments have an appreciable impact on current account balances: by 1985 the US current deficit would have been $27 billion smaller, at the expense of a $16 billion smaller surplus in Germany and a $10 billion reduction in the Japanese surplus. Indeed, by the final quarter of 1985, these figures were running at annual rates of $40 billion, $27 billion and $24 billion, respectively. Taking account of the J-curve and the rather moderate form of our policy reaction function, these results suggest that target zones would have worked in the expected way in a world described by the MCM.

TABLE C.2   **Impact of target zones and compensatory fiscal policy on key variables**

	1976	1977	1978	1979
United States				
Real GNP (percentage)	−0.0	−0.0	0.0	−0.0
Price level (percentage)	0.0	0.0	−0.0	−0.1
Interest rate (percentage points)	−0.2	−0.0	0.6	0.8
Real exchange rate (percentage)	−0.9	−0.3	1.7	2.4
Current balance (billion dollars)	0.1	0.9	1.1	−2.2
Canada				
Real GNP (percentage)	−0.0	−0.0	−0.0	−0.0
Price level (percentage)	0.4	0.1	−0.7	−1.5
Interest rate (percentage points)	−0.7	0.0	1.6	2.3
Real exchange rate (percentage)	−2.0	−0.6	4.0	6.8
Current balance (billion dollars)	−0.2	0.2	0.5	0.0
Germany				
Real GNP (percentage)	−0.0	−0.0	0.0	0.0
Price level (percentage)	−0.1	−0.1	0.2	0.8
Interest rate (percentage points)	0.1	0.0	−0.1	−0.4
Real exchange rate (percentage)	0.2	0.1	−0.4	−2.6
Current balance (billion dollars)	0.2	−0.2	−1.8	−0.1
Japan				
Real GNP (percentage)	−0.0	−0.0	−0.0	−0.0
Price level (percentage)	−0.1	0.1	0.3	−0.0
Interest rate (percentage points)	0.5	0.0	−1.5	−0.1
Real exchange rate (percentage)	1.5	−0.1	−5.1	−1.3
Current balance (billion dollars)	−0.2	−1.2	−1.6	6.9
United Kingdom				
Real GNP (percentage)	0.0	0.0	0.0	0.0
Price level (percentage)	−0.4	−0.4	−0.2	1.0
Interest rate (percentage points)	0.4	0.2	0.1	−0.8
Real exchange rate (percentage)	0.9	0.8	0.8	−2.9
Current balance (billion dollars)	0.5	−0.6	−1.2	−1.3

Note: Amounts shown are deviations from the baseline path.
Source: MCM.

1980	1981	1982	1983	1984	1985
−0.0	−0.0	−0.0	−0.0	−0.0	−0.0
−0.2	−0.2	−0.1	−0.0	0.2	0.6
0.6	−0.0	−0.4	−0.7	−2.2	−2.9
4.7	2.0	−0.9	−3.2	−8.7	−12.1
−6.9	−11.9	−8.4	−1.8	5.2	26.5
−0.0	−0.0	−0.0	−0.0	−0.0	−0.0
−1.6	−1.4	−1.0	−1.0	−1.5	−1.7
1.7	0.3	−0.0	−0.2	−0.2	−0.6
7.9	3.7	0.4	−1.3	−2.3	−3.6
−0.3	−0.9	−0.2	0.0	1.1	−0.7
−0.0	−0.0	−0.0	−0.0	−0.0	−0.0
0.8	−0.5	−1.0	−1.9	−3.6	−4.7
−0.2	1.7	1.8	2.7	4.3	4.3
−1.3	4.5	6.1	9.4	15.8	18.3
2.6	3.0	0.6	−2.2	−3.1	−15.6
−0.0	−0.0	−0.0	−0.0	−0.0	0.0
−0.1	−0.1	−0.2	−0.1	−0.1	0.0
0.2	−0.1	0.5	0.2	0.1	0.5
1.7	−0.2	0.8	−1.0	−1.5	−0.5
2.6	3.5	3.3	−1.0	0.4	−10.3
0.0	0.0	−0.0	−0.0	−0.0	−0.0
4.3	5.3	5.1	5.3	4.7	3.2
−3.7	−1.8	−0.4	0.1	0.7	0.8
−11.3	−10.6	−7.4	−5.3	−3.7	−1.7
−1.0	10.4	9.1	6.9	6.2	1.7

References

Adams, Charles, and Daniel Gros. 1986. "The Consequences of Real Exchange Rate Rules for Inflation." IMF *Staff Papers,* vol. 33, no. 2 (September).

Bergsten, C. Fred, and John Williamson. 1983. "Exchange Rates and Trade Policy." In *Trade Policy in the 1980s,* edited by William R. Cline. Washington: Institute for International Economics.

Bergsten, C. Fred. 1986a. "America's Unilateralism," In *Conditions for Partnership in International Economic Management.* C. Fred Bergsten, Etienne Davignon, and Isamu Miyazaki. The Triangle Papers: 32. New York, NY: Trilateral Commission.

———. 1986b. "Stabilizing the International Monetary System: The Case for Target Zones." In *Exchange Rate Targets: Desirable or Disastrous?,* edited by John H. Makin. AEI Studies 451. Washington: American Enterprise Institute for Public Policy Research.

Brittan, Samuel. 1987. *The Role and Limits of Government,* rev. ed. London: Wildwood House.

Bryant, Ralph; Dale W. Henderson; Gerald Holtham; Peter Hooper; and Steven A. Symansky, eds. *Empirical Macroeconomics for Interdependent Economies.* Washington: Brookings Institution, forthcoming.

Buiter, Willem H., and Richard Marston. 1985. *International Economic Policy Coordination.* Cambridge: Cambridge University Press.

Buiter, Willem H., and Marcus H. Miller. 1981. "The Thatcher Experiment: The First Two Years." *Brookings Papers on Economic Activity* 2.

Dornbusch, Rudiger, *Dollars, Debts, and Deficits.* 1986. Cambridge, Mass.: MIT Press.

———, "Why the Dollar Must Fall Another 30 Percent," *New York Times,* 10 May 1987.

Edison, Hali J.; Jaime R. Marquez, and Ralph W. Tryon. 1986. "The Structure and Properties of the FRB Multicountry Model." *International Finance Discussion Paper,* no. 293. Washington: Board of Governors of the Federal Reserve System, October.

Edison, Hali J., Marcus H. Miller, and John Williamson. 1987. "On Evaluating and Extending the Target Zone Proposal." *Journal of Policy Modeling,* no. 1.

Fischer, Stanley. 1986. "Time Consistent Fiscal and Monetary Policies: A Survey." Unpublished paper; processed.

Frenkel, Jacob A. 1987. "The International Monetary System: Should It Be Reformed?" *American Economic Review,* vol. 77, no. 2 (May).

Frenkel, Jacob A., and Morris Goldstein. 1986. "A Guide to Target Zones." IMF *Staff Papers,* vol. 33, no. 4 (December).

Friedman, Milton. 1953. "The Case for Flexible Exchange Rates." In Milton Friedman, *Essays in Positive Economics.* Chicago: University of Chicago Press.

———. 1968. "The Role of Monetary Policy." *American Economic Review,* vol. 58, no. 1 (March).

Giavazzi, Francesco, and Alberto Giovannini. 1987. "Models of the EMS: Is Europe a Greater Deutschemark Area?" January; processed.

Gordon, Robert J. 1985. "The Conduct of Domestic Monetary Policy." In *Monetary Policy in Our Times*, edited by Albert Ando et al. Cambridge, Mass.: MIT Press.

Group of 10. 1985. "The Functioning of the International Monetary System," Supplement to the *IMF Survey*, vol. 14 (July).

Grubb, David; Richard Jackman, and Richard Layard. 1982. "Causes of the Current Stagflation." *Review of Economic Studies*, vol. 49, no. 159.

Haberler, Gottfried. 1986. "The International Monetary System," *The AEI Economist*, July.

Halm, George N., ed. 1970. *Approaches to Greater Flexibility of Exchange Rates: The Bürgenstock Papers*. Princeton, NJ: Princeton University Press.

Johnson, Harry G. 1958. Towards a General Theory of the Balance of Payments. In Harry G. Johnson, *International Trade and Economic Growth*. London: Allen and Unwin.

Kenen, Peter B. 1987. "International Money and Macroeconomics." In *World Economic Problems*, edited by Kimberly A. Elliott and John Williamson. Washington: Institute for International Economics, forthcoming.

Kydland, Finn, and Edward Prescott. 1977. "Rules Rather Than Discretion: The Inconsistency of Optimal Plans." *Journal of Political Economy*, vol. 85.

Lucas, Robert E. 1981. "Econometric Policy Evaluation: A Critique." In Robert E. Lucas, *Studies in Business-Cycle Theory*. Cambridge, Mass.: MIT Press.

Marris, Stephen. 1987. *Deficits and the Dollar: The World Economy at Risk*, rev. ed. (1st. ed. 1985) POLICY ANALYSES IN INTERNATIONAL ECONOMICS 14. Washington: Institute for International Economics.

McKinnon, Ronald I. 1971. *Monetary Theory and Controlled Flexibility in the Foreign Exchanges*. Princeton Essays in International Finance no. 84. Princeton, NJ: International Finance Section, Department of Economics, Princeton University.

————. 1984. *An International Standard for Monetary Stabilization*. POLICY ANALYSES IN INTERNATIONAL ECONOMICS 8. Washington: Institute for International Economics.

————. "Monetary and Exchange Rate Policies for International Financial Stability: A Proposal," *Journal of Economic Perspectives*, forthcoming.

Meade, James E. 1984. "A New Keynesian Bretton Woods." *Three Banks Review*, June.

————. 1987. "Monetary Policy and Fiscal Policy: The Assignment of Weapons to Targets." Unpublished paper, June; processed.

Meese, Richard, and Kenneth Rogoff. 1983. "Empirical Exchange Rate Models of the 1970s: Do They Fit Out of Sample?" *Journal of International Economics*, vol. 13, no. 1/2 (February).

Miller, Marcus H. 1985. "Monetary Stabilization Policy in an Open Economy." *Scottish Journal of Political Economy*, vol. 32, no. 3 (November).

Miller, Marcus H., and John Williamson. "The International Monetary System: An Analysis of Alternative Regimes." *European Economic Review*, forthcoming.

Mundell, Robert A. 1968. *International Economics*. London: Macmillan.

————. 1971. *The Dollar and the Policy Mix*. Essays in International Finance, no. 85 (May). Princeton, NJ: International Finance Section, Department of Economics, Princeton University.

Oudiz, Gilles, and Jeffrey Sachs. 1984. "Macroeconomic Policy Coordination Among the Industrial Economies," *Brookings Papers on Economic Activity* 1.

Patinkin, Don. 1965. *Money, Interest, and Prices,* 2nd ed. New York, NY: Harper and Row.

Phelps, Edmund S. 1967. "Phillips Curves, Expectations of Inflation, and Optimal Unemployment over Time." *Economica,* vol. 34, no. 135 (August).

Phillips, A.W. 1954. "Stabilization Policy in a Closed Economy." *Economic Journal,* vol. 64, no. 254 (June)

———. 1958. "The Relation between Unemployment and the Rate of Change of Money Wages in the United Kingdom." *Economica,* vol. 25, no. 100 (November).

Poterba, James M., and Lawrence H. Summers. 1987. "Mean Reversion in Stock Returns: Evidence and Implications." Processed.

Rogoff, Kenneth. 1985. "Can International Monetary Policy Cooperation be Counterproductive?" *Journal of International Economics,* vol. 18, no. 314 (May).

Rosenbrock, H.H., and P.D. McMorran. 1971. "Good, Bad or Optimal." *IEEE Transactions in Automatic Control,* vol. AC16, no. 6.

Salmon, Mark, and Peter Young. 1979. "Control Methods and Quantitative Economic Policy." In *Optimal Control for Econometric Models,* edited by S. Holly, B. Rüstem, and M.B. Zarrop. London: Macmillan.

Solomon, Robert. 1987. Testimony before the U.S. Senate Foreign Relations Committee, Subcommittee on International Economic Policy, Trade, Oceans, and Environment, 20 March.

Stevens, Guy; Richard Berner; Peter Clark; Ernesto Fernandez-Cata; Howard Howe, and Sung Kwack. 1984. *The US Economy in an Interdependent World: A Multicountry Model.* Washington: Board of Governors of the Federal Reserve System.

Triffin, Robert. 1964. *The Evolution of the International Monetary System: Historical Reappraisal and Future Perspectives.* Studies in International Finance no. 12. Princeton, NJ: International Finance Section, Department of Economics, Princeton University.

Williamson, John. 1965. *The Crawling Peg.* Essays in International Finance no. 50. Princeton, NJ: International Finance Section, Department of Economics, Princeton University.

———. 1977. *The Failure of World Monetary Reform.* New York, NY: NYU Press.

———. 1981. *Exchange Rate Rules.* London: Macmillan.

———. 1985. *The Exchange Rate System,* rev. ed. (1st. ed. 1983). POLICY ANALYSES IN INTERNATIONAL ECONOMICS 5. Washington: Institute for International Economics.

———. 1986. "Target Zones and the Management of the Dollar." *Brookings Papers on Economic Activity* 1.

Wonnacott, Paul. 1987. *The United States and Canada: The Quest for Free Trade.* POLICY ANALYSES IN INTERNATIONAL ECONOMICS 16. Washington: Institute for International Economics.

Other Publications from the Institute

POLICY ANALYSES IN INTERNATIONAL ECONOMICS SERIES

BOOKS

SPECIAL REPORTS

FORTHCOMING